MW01077209

MAY 1959

As you can see in this photograph, Susan (she's the one in the front!) hung out in her grandparents' tavern at an early age. They taught her how to wash bar glasses, wipe the counter, and eventually how to drink . . . responsibly!

She doesn't claim to be an expert when it comes to Bloody Marys. . . . She just knows what she likes, and her choices in this guide represent those Bloodys that are delicious, nutritious, and amazing, in her opinion.

ADVENTURES ON THE BLOODY TRAIL: THE QUEST CONTINUES

BY SUSAN L. FIEBIG

DESIGN & ILLUSTRATION BY
JESSE ROELKE

Adventures on the Bloody Trail: The Quest Continues
Copyright © 2015, 2021 Susan Fiebig
ISBN 978-1-943331-12-3
Fifth Edition

Adventures on the Bloody Trail: The Quest Continues
by Susan Fiebig

Edited by Kaye Nemec
Design and Illustration by Jesse Roelke

For information, please contact:

www.ten16press.com
Waukesha, WI

The author has made every effort to ensure that the information within this book was accurate at the time of publication. The author does not assume and hereby disclaims any liability to any party for any loss, damage, or disruption caused by errors or omissions, whether such errors or omissions result from accident, negligence, or any other cause.

DEDICATION

I dedicate this book to all of you who followed *The Bloody Trail* in search of the best Wisconsin Bloody Marys.

Enjoy the Adventure!

ACKNOWLEDGEMENTS

Thank you to my family and friends who accompanied me on the numerous road trips throughout Wisconsin tasting Bloody Marys. I truly appreciate every one of you. To my publisher, Shannon, and all the great people at Ten16 Press for helping me meet my personal goals with this book. I couldn't have done it without you. And to Lauren whose expertise and patience made the challenge of revising *Adventures* a success. Cheers!

INTRODUCTION

When my first book, *The Bloody Trail: In Quest of the Best Wisconsin Bloody Marys*, was published in 2013, I had no idea that Bloodys were going to be so popular! I was lucky to have written my book just as the Bloody Mary craze began and I have enjoyed seeing this iconic cocktail become the center of attention at bars and restaurants throughout the country. Everyone began posting their favorite, over-the-top Bloody Marys on the internet . . . something I didn't see when I started this journey almost 14 years ago!

I met fabulous Bloody Mary lovers from all over the state and great people from as far away as Seattle (The Drunken Tomato, Demitri's BM Seasonings), Las Vegas (Bloody America), and Iowa (Benny's Original Meat Straws). Readers sent me recommendations, photos, and posts on my Facebook page about their favorite Bloody Mary venues. With everyone's help, I have had a fantastic ride on The Bloody Trail and this second book is filled with my adventures. I've added a list of Honorable Mentions because there are so many fantastic Bloody Marys in WI that even though they did not meet my criteria; they are still worth driving miles for.

I wish you happy trails and safe travels; but remember: Always assign a designated driver when you're on The Bloody Trail!

Cheers!
Susan

THE BLOODY CONTENTS

PEOPLE I'VE MET ALONG THE BLOODY TRAIL

MUST-SEE RESTAURANTS ALONG THE BLOODY TRAIL

THE BEST ON THE ROUTE

BON JOUR!

It all began here: a small bar in Paris, a French bartender, and thirsty patrons. Patrons who wanted something new, something different, something spicy! Bartender Fernand Petiot never hesitated when asked to concoct a new drink. He began with simple ingredients: the finest vodka to be found in Paris, freshly made tomato juice, and a bit of black pepper and Worcestershire sauce. Voila, the first Bloody Mary!

The bar is Harry's New York Bar at 5 Rue Daunou in Paris. Just another bar you say? Non, monsieur! Jockey Tod Sloan became partners with a New York City bar owner named Clancey, and opened Harry's on Thanksgiving Day in 1911. The interior of the bar was made with mahogany wood paneling and the counter was shipped from New York. Sloan hired a Scottish bartender, Harry MacElhone, to tend the bar on opening day; thus the name Harry's Bar. (See sidebar) It was often filled with expatriates from the United States escaping prohibition. In later years it catered to the elite of Paris. It is still in high demand today with mostly French businessmen relaxing after a long day at work.

The bar is quaint, a bit pretentious, and oftentimes so crowded you have to drink standing up. Here is where all the news of the day is discussed; politics abound and shouting above the noise of the tables of laughter is a normal occurrence. French is most often spoken here, but many world travelers have been drawn to Harry's Bar because of its notoriety. This was THE place to be seen and heard if you were anyone important in Paris. Ernest Hemingway frequented often and discussed his work with F. Scott Fitzgerald. George Gershwin was said to have written *An American in Paris* at Harry's Bar!

The bar remains the same today with an old style ambience . . . definitely not trendy in the least and all to the delight of patrons from all over the world.

scan me

To see Harry's New York Bar without spending all that cash on airfare, scan the QR code to the right.

SIDE BAR

Harry MacElhone was a well-known Scottish bartender of the day. He tended for a while in London where he published *Harry's ABC of mixing cocktails: Over 300 Cocktail Recipes*, by Harry MacElhone, 1921. Harry also bartended in the United States, at the Plaza in Manhattan, as well as in Southern France. He went on to write many more cocktail books during his lifetime, but interestingly with no mention of the Bloody Mary having been invented at his Paris bar. In fact, the nearest mention of the Bloody Mary in one of Harry's book is in the 1941 edition of his *ABC of mixing cocktails*, wherein he documents a vodka and tomato juice concoction called a "Red Mary."

SIDE BAR

Harry's conducts a straw poll before each US presidential election. Customers who provide proof of US citizenship can vote in the poll. The results have mirrored every election, except 1976 and 2004, since the poll began in 1924.

Cheers!
Au Revoir!

Update on the caretakers of Harry's New York Bar in Paris.

Harry MacElhone was born in Dundee in 1890 and was one of the first bartenders in Europe. He was asked to open the New York Bar in Paris (later to become Harry's New York Bar) in 1911, and he took over the ownership in 1923. During the first world war he served with the Royal Naval Air Service. During the second, the German invasion forced him to flee to London, but he returned to Paris in April 1945 and remained in charge of Harry's until his death in 1958.

Andrew MacElhone started working in Harry's Bar in 1939, at the age of 16. During the war years he worked in London bars before serving in the British Army and being severely wounded. He returned to Paris in 1947 and has remained at Harry's Bar ever since, although ill health has forced him to hand over the active running of the bar to his son.

Duncan MacElhone graduated from Georgetown University and worked in banking and finance before joining his father at Harry's Bar. He now looks after the management and day-to-day running of the bar, ensuring that it maintains the traditions and forward-looking character established by his grandfather.

To read much more about the history of Harry's New York Bar in Paris and about Harry MacElhone, go online and order your own copy of his book with new info by his son and grandson. There is so much more to the MacElhone/Harry's Bar story that can fit in this chapter. It truly is a landmark and **must-see** for everyone that visits Paris. The video gives you a look inside, but nothing will compare to really being there.

Cheers to Harry, Andrew and Duncan MacElhone!

Source: **Harry's ABC of of mixing cocktails** by Harry MacElhone,
with new material by Andrew and Duncan MacElhone; Souvenir Press 1996

ABOUT THAT FRENCH BARTENDER...

Now that you know something about Harry's New York Bar, and Harry himself, here's some info about Fernand Petiot, the man known for inventing the Bloody Mary. As in my first book, Petiot has always been credited with concocting the first Bloody Mary at Harry's Bar. As you will read later, there are contradictions to this account.

Yes, Fernand Petiot was one of the first bartenders to work with Harry MacElhone in his newly acquired Paris bar, however he did not stay long, deciding to move to America in 1925. David Wondrich, author of two cocktail books and cocktail writer for US Esquire magazine, confirms the year was 1925 when Petiot arrived In America and that he moved to Ohio in 1928.

From the January 8th, 1975 edition of the Ohio Newspaper:
"Petiot was born Feb. 18, 1900, in Paris, and began his bartending career at Harry's Bar in Paris -- a tavern frequented by American celebrities and journalists -- and came to Ohio in 1928 as assistant manager of the Canton Club, a businessman's luncheon club."

What is so important about the above information is that it contradicts the myth that Petiot went straight from Harry's New York Bar to the St. Regis Hotel in 1933, upon the repeal of Prohibition (1920-1933). And so it was at the repeal of Prohibition in 1933 that Fernand Petiot finally moved to New York City, to become head bartender and beverage and wine cellar manager at the St. Regis Hotel.

Okay, so this isn't such a big deal, right? So he didn't go straight to New York from Paris . . . he STILL made the darn Bloody at the St. Regis Hotel, right?!

Here's his recipe and I rest my case! This specific recipe was used at the King Cole Room, which Ferdinand Petiot refers to, was chronicled in 'Crosby Gaige's Cocktail Guide and Ladies' Companion.' (1941), under the name of "Red Snapper".

RED SNAPPER (1941)

1 1/2 ounces tomato juice
1 1/2 ounces vodka
2 dashes Worcestershire sauce
2 dashes fresh lemon juice
Salt to taste
Cayenne pepper to taste

Combine all ingredients. Shake, then strain into a chilled cocktail glass.

Cheers, Fernand!

KING COLE BAR, ST. REGIS HOTEL IN NEW YORK CITY

In 1932, the iconic "Old King Cole" painting by Maxfield Parrish, which had been created for Astor's defunct Knickerbocker Hotel, was moved to the St. Regis and made the centerpiece of a new bar, the King Cole Bar, which has remained a New York institution ever since. Two years later, in 1934, bartender Fernand Petiot invented a drink there which he called the "Red Snapper". It has since become known around the world as the Bloody Mary.

The Maxfield Parrish mural was originally commissioned in 1906 by hotel owner John Jacob Astor for his 42nd Street hotel, The Knickerbocker. But that place was short-lived and after Astor perished on the Titanic in 1912, the mural eventually made its home in the St. Regis. In the first year of the bar, only men were permitted to enjoy the plush surroundings. Finally, in 1950, women joined the revelry under the watchful eye of Old King Cole.

For decades, King Cole has been delighting patrons, including Salvador Dali, Marilyn Monroe, Joe DiMaggio, and John Lennon. It has been featured in several movies including The Devil Wears Prada, Hannah and Her Sisters, and The First Wives' Club. In 2007, the 30' x 8' mural received a $100,000 cleaning which completely restored the beloved masterpiece to its original splendor.

Forbes Magazine's Richard Nalley, Editor-At-Large, wrote in his article, **Legends of Old King Cole at the St. Regis:**

". . . John Jacob Astor begged and wheedled the famous painter and illustrator Maxfield Parrish to paint the King Cole mural for his Knickerbocker Hotel, eventually offering him an unheard of sum of $5,000. But the relationship of the two strong personalities was fraught from the beginning, and after much to-ing and fro-ing the gorgeous mural was delivered in 1906 with a subtle thumb to Astor's eye. Look up at the mural today and it's easy to believe the story is true: King Cole is said to be the sour likeness of Astor himself, and his courtiers, suppressing laughter all around him, have just heard him fart."

This makes the trip here so much more memorable and I cannot help but laugh along with his courtiers!

ERNEST HEMINGWAY AND THE BLOODY MARY

Ernest Hemingway, famous author and master drinker, was a regular at Harry's New York Bar in Paris. He was often seen throwing back a few with composer George Gershwin and fellow writer F. Scott Fitzgerald. I am sure he was also spotted sitting alone while possibly contemplating his next book with a Bloody Mary in front of him! But, Ernest Hemingway was also interested in the making of the Bloody Mary and, as a tribute to the way he lived; he created his own larger than life version. He didn't much care for all of those extra fancy ingredients. He kept it simple, like his writing style.

Ernest sent this recipe to Bernard Peyton on April 5, 1947:

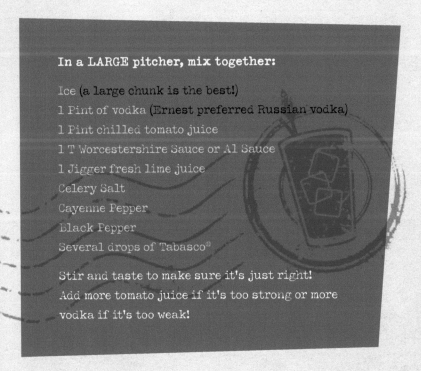

In a LARGE pitcher, mix together:

Ice (a large chunk is the best!)
1 Pint of vodka (Ernest preferred Russian vodka)
1 Pint chilled tomato juice
1 T Worcestershire Sauce or A1 Sauce
1 Jigger fresh lime juice
Celery Salt
Cayenne Pepper
Black Pepper
Several drops of Tabasco®

Stir and taste to make sure it's just right!
Add more tomato juice if it's too strong or more vodka if it's too weak!

He goes on to say, "For combating a really terrific hangover increase the amount of Worcestershire sauce — but don't lose the lovely color. Keep drinking it yourself to see how it is doing. After you get the hang of it you can mix it so it will taste as though it had absolutely no alcohol of any kind in it and a glass of it will still have as much kick as a really good, big martini. Whole trick is to keep it very cold and not let the ice water it down."

The U.S. Treasury Department hired Ernest Hemingway as a spy in China in 1941. Ernest just happened to be in the area honeymooning with his wife, Martha Gellhorn. The great literary man of action reveled in being a government operative, while his journalist wife championed the anti-Japanese resistance of Chiang Kai-shek.

There is speculation that Ernest Hemingway and his wife were the first to discover the Bloody Mary. Or perhaps they concocted the drink while traveling (and spying) in China where vodka may have been available, but there wasn't much to mix it with except tomato juice. There's not too much in the history books about what Ernest and Martha did with their free time, so we will just have to assume that this happened. There is some proof to the story found in a letter Hemingway wrote to a friend. "I introduced this drink (Bloody Mary) to Hong Kong in 1941 and believe it did more than any other single factor except perhaps the Japanese Army to precipitate the fall of that Crown Colony!"

Did I read anywhere that Ernest taught Fernand Petiot how to make the drink while sitting at Harry's Bar? Does it really matter? I think not! What matters is that we all enjoy a good story while sipping a great Bloody Mary and that's what this book is all about.

·ERNEST· HEMINGWAY

Here's a reminder from my first book on how I score Bloody Marys. You can take it or leave it! I know what I like and I think you will too!

THE BLOODY CRITERIA

 Glass: A simple pint beer glass is preferred.

Celery Salt: On the rim of the glass.

Shaken: With the use of a cocktail shaker.

Veggies: At least 4 are preferred, more is better, variety is crucial.

Beer: Size is everything.

Taste: Mix or from scratch, taste is King.

Presentation: Overall appearance of the delivery.

When judging a Bloody using my criteria, please note that I am generous as long as the Bloody tastes good and the atmosphere is pleasant. The ambience of the establishment can make or break a good score, as does the personality of the bartender. But ultimately it is the drink that gets the final score. A good Bloody can often erase a poor dining experience.

 First, a Bloody should always be served in a tall glass. This is better for overall presentation but also because, if the drink tastes good, I always want more. I have yet to order a second Bloody, as a good one is usually enough, and a bad one is usually left behind!

 Celery salt is most often added to the mix, but a good Bloody will have celery salt around the rim; the saltier the better!

 A great bartender knows the importance of using a shaker to stir his/ her drinks. A great Bloody is ALWAYS stirred or, better yet, shaken. Often, if there is an audience, the bartender will make a spectacle of the procedure and pour one mix into another glass and back again. This always gets the Bloody a higher score.

Now to the veggie score! This is so very important and is, unfortunately, often overlooked. Even a great-tasting Bloody will not score high if the veggies are scarce. I prefer, at the very least, a pickle, celery stalk, and two olives. Anything less is just not worthy of a good score. The high scorers in this book demonstrate going over the top! Notice how the addition of a sausage stick, string cheese, or shrimp increases the rating. I always say, "A Bloody Mary should be an appetizer to a good meal!"

There has been a resurgence of the Bloody Mary cocktail in local bars and restaurants in the last 5+ years, creating a competition between establishments. Many enterprising owners have added sliders, brats, shrimp or a thick slice of bacon with the veggie list! BONUS! I always enjoy an appetizer in my Bloodys, and now it is becoming standard procedure.

When it comes to the beer chaser, well, that is always your preference. (It constitutes another book—but there are already plenty of them out there about BEER! I will not even go there!) Sorry, but in this case, size does matter! A beer chaser means two things (at least in Wisconsin): FREE and BIG! For a good score, I demand a 6 oz. beer, at least. It has to look good sitting next to that 12 oz. Bloody Mary. I have seen the cute little beer mugs and miniature beer glasses, and although charming, they just don't add up. Give me a beer that matches the Bloody, or you will score low! This is often the high-score breaker, even with a great-tasting Bloody. And if you cannot give me a free beer, then don't bother at all!

Overall taste of the Bloody cannot be overlooked and will oftentimes make what might be a poor score a bit better. Nothing beats a tasty special mix made right at the bar each night. From experience, I do not get the secret easily, but I have prodded a few from personable bartenders. It could be just adding a bit o' Guinness or Worcestershire sauce that makes a good drink. Clamato juice is often used, especially at seafood restaurants. The most popular ingredient in house mixes is the TABASCO® brand Pepper Sauce by McIlhenny Company. It has been around since 1868 and continues to add a little spice to one's life. One restaurant served a miniature bottle of TABASCO® with each Bloody Mary! Very good move!!! I also love the addition of horseradish to the mix. This gives the Bloody a sassy bite that keeps you on your toes. Spice is nice!

Now down to the last criteria: overall presentation. All of the above components of a good Bloody make for a high score. Let's review:

* Large glass—the bigger the better

* Celery salt rubbed along the rim of the glass.

* Shaken—preferably with a cocktail shaker.

* Lots and lots of veggies—throw in a
  Slim Jim® or shrimp!

* Beer—big and beautiful, your choice.

* Taste—spicy and flavorful

There you have it! All of these criteria make for a beautiful presentation. They work together to create the perfect Bloody Mary . . . or at least a high-scoring one.

THE BLOODY SCORE

A word on consistency . . . don't hold me to the score if the bartender is having a bad day or if a different, or even new (just graduated from mixology college), bartender is at the helm. Or perhaps a new "secret" recipe is being tried out on the clientele. In any case, give the place a chance and try it again.

It wouldn't be in this book if it wasn't great at least twice for THIS veteran Bloody drinker. Variables do occur, and one must always give an establishment a second chance. Do not judge the drink by poor service, an unhappy bartender, or bad timing all the way around. Sit back and enjoy the drink! And don't forget to ask if that Bloody comes with a beer chaser!

POINTS	CATEGORY	SCORE
4	Glass	
2	Celery salt	
3	Shaken	
10	Veggies	
6	Presentation	
15	Taste	
10	BeerChaser	
50	Total	

How To Mix a Bloody Mary
— (in 6 STEPS) —

1. Ingredients:
Salt & pepper
Tomato Juice
worchestershire
(scale down)

2.

3.

4.

5.

6. (final product)

The Bloody Mary has the reputation of being a cure for a hangover. This makes the cocktail a popular beverage in the morning and early afternoon, especially with brunch. Unfortunately, a Bloody Mary only numbs the pain of a hangover; but a great Bloody Mary can put a smile on your face!

The Bloody Mary is not a complex drink: vodka and tomato juice; but there are many variations on this theme. Here are more versions that may pique your interest.

BLOODY BEER
Beer, usually a light beer or lager, replacing vodka. Often served with Worcestershire sauce, black pepper, hot sauce, and/or lime

BLOODY BISHOP
Sherry in equal measure to vodka

BLOODY BOYARSKY
Grenadine, Tabasco®, vodka

BLOODY CAB
Cabernet Sauvignon replacing/in addition to the vodka

BLOODY CAESAR
Clamato juice, hot sauce, salt and pepper and Worcestershire sauce

BLOODY DERBY
Bourbon replacing vodka

BLOODY FAIRY, RED FAIRY
Absinthe replacing the vodka

BLOODY GEISHA, BLOODY NINJA
Sake replacing vodka

BLOODY HILLBILLY
Moonshine replacing vodka

BLOODY HOGGER
Bacon Vodka replacing vodka

BLOODY JERRY
Replace vodka with Madra Rua Irish Pub's Heady Veggie Vodka or any other veggie

Infused vodka and add 1 pull (approximately 1/2 ounce) of Guinness. A variation created by a long term customer of the Pub

BLOODY EIGHT OR EIGHT BALL
Replace tomato juice with V8 vegetable juice

BLOODY LEROY
Replace tomato juice with barbecue sauce

BLOODY MAUREEN
Replace vodka with Guinness

BLOODY MOLLY
Replace vodka with Irish whiskey

BROWN MARY
Replace vodka with any whiskey

BLOODY MOO MOO
Replace vodka with milk (really?!?!?!)

BLOODY MURDER
Gin, black vinegar, and wasabi sauce

BLOODY PHILLIP
80-proof rice distilled liquor from Thailand replaces vodka

BLOODY PIRATE
Cubanito, dark rum, replaces vodka

BLOODY SCOTSMAN
Replace vodka with Scotch whiskey

BLOODY SUNSHINE
Habanera sauce replaces Tabasco®

DANISH MARY OR BLOODY DANE
Replace vodka with aquavit

MICHELADA
Mexican beer replaces vodka; beer equals tomato juice

VIRGIN MARY, BLOODY SHAME, BLOODY VIRGIN, OR BLOODY BARBARA
No alcohol

The following variations use vodka but change the mixer:

BLOODY BLACKIE
Coca-cola instead of tomato juice—but that just isn't right!

BLOODY BULL
Beef bouillon and tomato juice.

BLOODY CARY
Carrot juice instead of tomato juice

BLOODY EIGHT OR EIGHT BALL
V8 replaces tomato juice

BLOODY LEROY
Barbecue sauce replace tomato juice

BLOODY MARIYAKI
Teriyaki sauce instead

I just had my first **TRUE BLOOD** here in Fond du Lac at O'Davey's! That was after I had my Sarah Jayne Pickart Bloody Mary! The True Blood uses Jagermeister instead of vodka along with a lot of Tabasco® and tomato juice. I actually liked it . . . a lot!

Here are some variations of the drink format:

FROZEN BLOODY MARY
Blend it like you would a margarita

BLOODY MARGARET
Same as above but add milk when you serve it . . . inspired by the Orange Julius

FLAMING BLOODY MARY
Add a small amount of 151 rum on the top; place a string on it and let it hang off the side of the glass. Then ignite it! This is for the magician in all of us! Try it for July4th!

BLOODY MARYNARA
Use marinara instead of tomato juice but serve it in a shot glass

SCREW MARY
Equal parts vodka, orange juice and tomato juice

BLOODY MARY-LAND OR CRABBY MARY
Use Old Bay Seasoning instead of celery salt

And for all the naughty Bloody Mary lovers:

SLUTTY MARY
Garnish with a sausage!

BLOODY CHARLIE
Garnish with two olives!

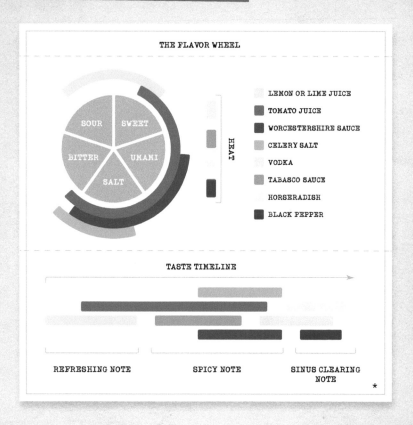

THE FLAVOR WHEEL

SOUR SWEET
BITTER UMAMI
SALT

HEAT

LEMON OR LIME JUICE
TOMATO JUICE
WORCESTERSHIRE SAUCE
CELERY SALT
VODKA
TABASCO SAUCE
HORSERADISH
BLACK PEPPER

TASTE TIMELINE

REFRESHING NOTE   SPICY NOTE   SINUS CLEARING
NOTE
★

This chapter is for those Bloody Mary Lovers who enjoy chemistry, analysis and technology. If you aren't one of these 'geeks' you can skip this chapter; but I recommend you go for it. You may learn a few things about Bloodys that will make you go "Hmmmmm!"

Hemingway's recipe involved a lot of "tasting-as-you-go," and a long list of ingredients: vodka, tomato juice, Worcestershire sauce, lime juice, celery salt, cayenne pepper (modern bartenders usually substitute Tabasco®) and black pepper.

"Each of those ingredients has tens of compounds, if not hundreds of compounds," Neil Da Costa, an analytic chemist working for International Flavors and Fragrances says. "The bloody mary has been called the world's most complex cocktail."

He should know. Da Costa has used every trick in the chemist's book to analyze each ingredient, and the cocktail as a whole. He presented his findings at a meeting of the American Chemical Society. Da Costa, an expert in food flavors, is chairman-elect of the group's agriculture and food chemistry division.

With gas and liquid chromatography, Da Costa isolated the wide variety of compounds that give the Bloody Mary its unique flavor. The drink covers much of the taste spectrum: sweet, salty, sour and umami—the savory taste of glutamic acid.

*A visualization of the flavors in a typical Bloody Mary. This diagram, by NPR's Adam Cole, is based on the research of Neil Da Costa, a chemist who specializes in the chemical analysis. Heavy stuff, isn't it? But, informative. Here's more on the subject:

Da Costa's research provides many insights for making a good Bloody Mary:

* **MAKE IT FRESH.** Chemically, the Bloody Mary is a "highly unstable" concoction, and the quality tends to deteriorate quickly.

* **ICE IT UP.** Serving Bloody Marys on ice helps to slow down the chemical reactions involving acids in tomato juice and other ingredients that degrade the taste.

* **MIND YOUR MIXES.** If you use a cocktail mix, add some fresh ingredients to enhance the flavor and aroma.

* **SPLURGE ON THE JUICE.** Tomato juice makes up most of the Bloody Mary's volume, so use high quality juice that has a deep, rich flavor.

* **ECONOMIZE ON THE VODKA.** The intense, spicy flavor of a Bloody Mary masks the vodka, and using premium vodka makes little sense.

I am not sure I agree with all of Dr. Da Costa's recommendations, but I certainly like the idea that drinking a Bloody Mary can be beneficial to the body! **Cheers to that!**

I received a Facebook message from Ron Hurm from Appleton, WI. He asked if I had heard of the term 'snit'?! I had not, so I decided to research it and found some great information. It is derived from U.S. dialect, so be proud people! We have created a word all by ourselves that doesn't come from some foreign country!

Here's what 'snit' means:

1. A U.S. unit of volume for liquor equal to 2 jiggers, 3 U.S. fluid ounces, or 88.7 milliliters.

2. (U.S., dialect) A beer chaser commonly served in three ounce servings in highball or juice glasses with a Bloody Mary cocktail in the upper Midwest states of United States including Minnesota, Wisconsin, Iowa, and Illinois.

Ex: "The bartender served us each a snit with our Bloody Marys this morning."

THE HISTORY OF THE SNIT

Posted on February 4, 2012 by Sarah Roettger, brunchkateers.com

If you are wondering about the amount of beverages included in some of the brunch pictures, there's a story about that. Ideally you should have 5 glasses in front of you: water, coffee, Bloody Mary, free mimosa, and your snit. Your what? In the upper Midwest region, chiefly Minnesota and Wisconsin, we are accustomed to getting a small beer with our Bloody Marys, called a snit. Here's the story:

In the 1950's vodka was scarce in the US mostly due to some shenanigans in Russia. Because of this, a relatively new drink, the Bloody Mary, was missing a main ingredient. Minnesotans, long known for their heartiness, gumption, and fondness for plaid, did not take well to the idea of not enjoying a Bloody Mary before going out to cut massive ice cubes out of the lakes. Creatively, they began making Bloody Marys with beer, something that was not experiencing a supply problem. Likely they used Hamm's or Grain Belt or other locally available beers.

But here's the thing. The cans were typically 10 or 12 oz. of beer. To ensure ideal deliciousness of your Bloody Mary, you don't want the entire beer in your drink. Minnesotans are also, let's say "thrifty." They wouldn't want the extra beer just tossed out or wasted somehow. So the bartender would empty the rest of the beer can into a 'lowball' or large shot glass and serve it to you with your Bloody Mary. *Cue angelic singing* the snit is born.

1 Coffee 2 Water 3 Bloody Mary 4 Snit 5 Mimosa

At least, that's the story I've heard and possibly embellished. If you've heard differently, let me know!

Next time you order your Bloody Mary at your favorite pub or restaurant, ask for a snit to go with your Bloody and see what happens. I am sure it will create quite a stir with the other guests and you will be the expert on the snit! Cheers!

THE TAPPER

Remember the name of that perfect size beer poured right from the tap? You know what I'm talking about . . . you're sitting at your favorite local tavern and the bar keep is entertaining you with stories of long ago, or the latest in weather or sports. Yeah, that cold glass of beer on the bar in front of you is often called a chaser (especially to seasoned Bloody Mary lovers like yourself). But those of us old enough to know better remember its original name, the 'tapper.' All taverns served tappers in an 8 oz. glass or even a 'cheater glass' that looked the same but only held 7 oz. (whatever!) Back then bartenders made sure each patron had a cold tapper in front of them at all times AND if the conversation was interesting, he would pour you your 3rd tapper on the house (free of charge, people)!

You would leave with one under your belt, or perhaps a second if you had a long day at the office or running around with the kiddos. And that was all you needed. You'd head home for dinner with the family or to walk the dog before reclining in your favorite chair to watch TV! Ah yes, those were the days!

Archie Bunker

But, you just don't see tappers served like that anymore. The type of tavern that serves tappers isn't common unless you travel away from the big cities and find yourself in a Wisconsin hamlet with a church and two bars. They are still out there, people. Trust me! And YES, they serve tappers but usually not a very good Bloody. But we aren't talking about Bloody Marys right now! This is about that 8 oz. beer! Even though the tapper is the perfect size chaser for a Bloody, most places have forgotten that rule and give you a beer in a cute little mug or glass. (There are some bars that serve a PINT glass of beer with their Bloodys and to them I say, "Bravo!")

There isn't a good Wikipedia definition of a tapper to be found, only discussions about the equipment necessary to tap a keg. Those of you who fondly recall a tapper probably have at least one glass in your cupboard (I know I do!). They're the perfect size for those occasions when one beer is just enough. Check out your local bar supply store and ask for a tapper glass. My local shop owner knew exactly what I wanted; of course, she owned a bar for over 30 years!

Cheers to those hidden taverns along the back roads of Wisconsin who still serve tappers!

And Cheers to my chiropractor, Andrew Judkins, for bringing up this subject at my last adjustment!

scan me

HOW TO POUR A TAPPER

Check out this video. It shows you how to pour the perfect pint, but it will certainly work for pouring the perfect tapper too!

PEOPLE I'VE MET ALONG
THE BLOODY TRAIL

MY BIG FAT BLOODY MARY A.K.A. GREG TOOKE

While exploring the internet in search of other Bloody Mary enthusiasts, I found an interesting site. I really didn't know who the person behind the MBFBM name or under the paper bag was, but I liked his style. He obviously loved Bloody Marys . . . well, more like he was infatuated with them. NO, I think OBSESSED is the right word!

Curiosity got the best of me, so I started a conversation with him and sent him a copy of my first book, *The Bloody Trail: In Quest of the Best Wisconsin Bloody Marys*. He not only liked it, he reviewed it on one of his weekly podcasts, where he discusses the Bloody Mary life.

After many discussions online, Greg invited me to his home for his twice-monthly Bloody Mary parties! He opens his home to guests, makes gallons of homemade Bloody Marys using Greg's own infused vodkas, creates a table of garnishes ranging from thick-sliced bacon, cheeses, and every pickled produce you can imagine! AND there's usually a live band hanging out in his living room for these Bloody events. On very special occasions, Greg will grab his guitar and sing a few ballads. All the Bloodys you would want to drink and great company to boot! Greg is the lead singer in the local La Crosse band, Big Liquor (appropriately named)! Look them up on YouTube!

Greg travels a lot and everywhere he goes, he orders a Bloody and posts photos on his website and Facebook page. Sometimes he posts 2-3 different Bloody photos in one day! That IS an obsession.

La Crosse, Wisconsin is noted for having the most bars on a main street! There's a bar or restaurant every few hundred yards so there's always room for everyone to enjoy a cocktail and a great meal. And on a weekend night, the streets are full of college students and regular folk too! (If you're looking for a traditional Wisconsin street party, go to La Crosse for Octoberfest and you will not be disappointed!)

But even though the bars are plentiful, Greg was never satisfied with the quality of the Bloody Marys served. During his college years (1983-4), he frequented The

Stateroom, still located at 128 3rd St. Their slogan states, "Having a good time The Old Fashioned Way!" They served Bloodys during Happy Hour for $2 back then and Greg thought THAT was way too pricey for the quality of the cocktail served! They were not tasty enough and were served in a mug . . . WHAT?!

After many over-engineered tries to make the perfect Bloody, Greg searched online and found Ernest Hemingway's original recipe and that's where he started. Using Hemingway's recipe, he experimented with various ingredients to come up with his very own delicious mix. He uses many of his own home-grown veggies to make fantastic seasonings for the rim of the glass—a perfect combination. He also has a passion for infusing vodkas with just about anything from his backyard garden.

Check out Greg's website and Facebook page for lots of interesting Bloody Mary facts and more!

www.mybigfatbloodymary.com
www.facebook.com/MyBigFatBloodyMary

Greg enjoys sharing his tips, his reviews of bottled Bloody Mary mixes, and his likes and dislikes of various venues throughout the state who serve Bloodys. Just follow his Facebook page or website and you will have access to all his YouTube videos. Greg is a judge at many national Bloody Mary competitions and promotes "better living through better cocktails." There's a lot of crazy Bloody Mary connoisseurs out there, but this writer thinks Greg is the MASTER OF HIS OWN (BLOODY MARY) DOMAIN!

Cheers Greg!

7 WAYS TO RUIN A BLOODY MARY

By Greg Tooke

After interviewing Greg Tooke, I got his permission to reprint his excellent article about the importance of the Bloody Mary drink itself. "It seems that every restaurant, bar, tailgater, and foodie across this great land is in a competition to craft the Best Bloody Mary. Garnishes tower like monuments to false gods and seasonings and mixes pile up like train wrecks. It's as if a fourth year engineering student decided to take up chemistry as a hobby."

I do believe that in my first book, *The Bloody Trail: In Quest of the Best Wisconsin Bloody Marys*, I stressed the importance of ALL THE CRITERIA to make a really great Bloody. Of course, garnishes are rated high, but the overall taste of the Bloody is of utmost importance. Greg agrees with me.

Here are his "SEVEN DEADLY BLOODY MARY SINS" with a few of my comments:

 "Fail to thoroughly mix it. Take the time to mix it thoroughly." I believe shaking or tossing it back and forth from one glass to the next is the best way to accomplish this.

 "Don't chill it. Fill the glass with ice and let it do its job! A properly chilled drink retains its flavor and is more pleasing to the palate than one matching your body temperature."

 "Over-engineer it. You've probably experienced this. Some ham-handed bartender gets a hold of a few too many ingredients and the next thing you know you're drinking steak sauce and rose petals. KEEP IT SIMPLE!"

 "Make a large batch days in advance. Bars are usually the culprit on this one, but an over-anxious tailgater might do it too. Mixing the ingredients long before consuming them allows the acids in tomato juice to start breaking down the flavors." Although I do agree with Greg's theory here, in my last book, Wicked Hop owner Miles stated that they do mix up a large batch of their Bloody Mary mix ahead of time and keep it chilled. I have never had a bad tasting Bloody at their establishment. Perhaps they have a special method that they are keeping to themselves.

 "Use a store-bought pre-mix. Admittedly, there are times when the convenience of a mix is too hard to resist, but think of these like TV dinners. They should not be your go-to solution." I agree here, but I have found some really good bottled Bloody Mary mixes. When forced to recommend a bottle mix, I usually suggest Zing-Zang. Lots of bars use it and it has a great taste all by itself. Yes, making your own mix is best, but sometimes you just want to stir up a Bloody really quickly without the hassle of making it from scratch.

"Become so obsessed with constructing an AMUSEMENT PARK on top of your drink that you forget the basics. I don't care how many exotic cuisines and movie tickets your Bloody Mary boasts. If the drink sucks, you've wasted time, energy, and money. We call this practice GARNOUFLAGE!"

Agreed, Mr. Tooke; however, once again there are always exceptions to the rule. Sarah Jayne Pickart of O'davey's Pub in Fond du Lac is well-known for her over-the-top artistic creations and Wild and Crazy Bloody Marys, AND she makes her own mix with 37 different ingredients, some of which are not even from this country! I feel she has found the right combination of garnouflage and Bloody Mary mix to override this deadly sin! But I know you appreciate her style and Sarah Jayne is often a guest at your Bloody Mary events, so I forgive you!

7 DEADLY BLOODY MARY SINS

"Withhold or charge extra for a beer chaser. If you must build the added cost of a beer chaser into your price, then do it. To skip this valuable component of the experience is sloppy, and to charge extra for it is offensive." Absolutely true!!!! As one of the criteria for a high-rated Bloody Mary states in my book: Give us a beer that matches the Bloody or you will score low! And if you cannot give us a free beer, then don't bother at all! This is often the high-score breaker even with a great tasting Bloody.

MAKING COCKTAILS SPECIAL

Much ado has been made of bloody Mary garnishes this year. Every couple of weeks a story seems to pop up in the news about the most outrageous bloody Mary. The west coast has their opulent brunch specials with bloody Mary bars that offer more food choices than an all you can eat dinner buffet. The eastern and southern coasts have tall hurricane glasses with shrimp and all manner of seafood as bloody Mary garnishes. But nowhere does the garnish of a bloody Mary become more ridiculous, more over the top, and more outrageous than in the Midwest, most specifically, Wisconsin.

As a native Midwesterner and aficionado of the tomato brunch cocktail, I've had the pleasure to sample many of these works of art. From the simple celery stalk to the towering tree of bloody Mary fruit served at O'Davey's Irish Pub & Restaurant in Fond du Lac, Wisconsin. I've come to appreciate a good garnish, but also to learn its place.

Before breaking down and listing the essential elements of good bloody Mary garnishes, let's put things in perspective. We're making/ordering/drinking a cocktail here. So before we go dressing up the little tart, let's make sure that she is of good stock. There's nothing worse than paying $20.00 for some towering abomination, only to find that the bar or restaurant has used some cheap mix to craft the cocktail, a practice I call, "garnouflage." Don't try hiding a poor bloody Mary behind licorice ropes and pinwheels. Start with a good solid bloody Mary recipe.

So you have a good fresh drink. Great! Now it's time to make a statement, provide a little extra nourishment, and give folks something to talk about and share with friends. Much of what makes bloody Mary garnishes great is the same as what makes a bloody Mary great; fresh ingredients, proper food handling, and presentation. Your aunt's pickled turtle eggs might be the talk of the town, but no one is going to share a picture of it on Facebook if it's sunk to the bottom of their drink. Get those garnishes up where we can see them. Using a skewer and resting the goodies on top of the glass lets the whole world see your art, and also saves room in the glass for the main attraction: The bloody Mary.

If your get together, restaurant, or bar has a theme, go with it. If you're in Wisconsin, include cheese and sausage. If you're at a beach party, add some shrimp. If you're trying to promote your pirate themed eatery, skewer veggies on a hook. You get the idea: make it fun, interesting, and memorable.

Keep your bloody Mary garnishes properly stored or refrigerated until using. Seeing a 5 gallon bucket of pre-skewered cheese and wilted pickle sitting out in a smoky bar is disgusting Keep it fresh!

Our Picks for Top Garnish Honors:

* **CELERY** This is the time-honored classic. The flavor compliments any bloody Mary, and those green leaves are an iconic symbol of daytime drinking.

* **PICKLE** Pickles store well, and offer as many variations as the drink itself. Homemade is best. Never serve them wilted.

* **OLIVES** Again, they keep well, and most homes and bars have them on hand. They're always a good complement to vodka.

* **PEPPERONCINI PEPPERS** A little sour, a little spicy, and a little salty like a good bloody Mary should be. Perfect. Their lighter color also makes for good accent.

* **BEEF STICK** 'nuff said

* **PEPPER-JACK CHEESE** Yes, I'm from Wisconsin.

I consider these bloody Mary garnishes to be the first tier. Here are a few secondary possibilities please add your own: Beef jerky, shrimp, polish sausage, asparagus (pickled or fresh), cucumber, bacon, lemon and lime wedges, pickled eggs, pickled brussels sprouts.

Cheers!
Greg

SARAH JAYNE + BLOODY MARYS = ART

When I first began my search for the best Bloody Marys in Wisconsin, I saw an image of a Brewers Bloody Mary created by Sarah Jayne Pickart of Fond du Lac on the popular nationally syndicated website, Thrillist. Her fabulous creations were featured on their page and viewers from all over the U.S. responded with, "We want more!" Sarah did not disappoint! Search for 'Sarah Jayne Pickart's Brewers Bloody Mary' and more about her and her amazing Bloodys at **www.thrillist.com**.

Sarah Jayne's story starts at O'davey's Pub located in downtown Fond du Lac; a bar owned and operated by a woman! Cheers to that! Sarah Jayne Pickart is passionate . . . I mean PASSIONATE about Bloody Marys. A Bloody Mary is her canvas where she creates beautifully orchestrated masterpieces of drink, food and fun! She can take a pint glass and transform it into a bountiful feast of goodies no Bloody, or human being, has ever seen before!

Even though Sarah Jayne has a degree in Cosmetology, she has tended bar for over 12 years and is an expert mixologist. She learned the foundation for creating Bloody Marys from scratch while tending bar at a popular Friday night fish fry restaurant located along beautiful Lake Winnebago.

When I asked her how her love for Bloody Mary creations started, she said it all began with a martini! Wait. . . A MARTINI!!?? Over several years, Sarah Jayne created a menu of 100 original martinis complete with fancy garnishes such as hard candies and frozen desserts on a swizzle stick balanced on the martini glass. One of her creations is the S'Mores martini seen here. Another specialty is her fresh fruit mojitos especially popular in the summer. Sarah Jayne continues to experiment with cocktail transformations and patrons to O'davey's are always excited to see what she is going to create next!

Her passion for Bloody Marys began on a quiet Sunday morning in October of 2011, while working at O'davey's.

The Bloody Mary was not a drink Sarah Jayne highlighted in her repertoire of signature cocktails, but the idea of making over-the-top garnishes to compliment the drink started her wild and crazy imagination flowing! Within a few minutes she had designed six Bloody Mary creations: The Italian, The Fiesta, Run It Through the Garden, The Irish, The Southern, and the now famous Wisconsin Game Day Bloody Mary. The next week, Sarah Jayne posted a special, "$2.50 Wild and Crazy Bloody Mary Day" on the door of O'davey's and well . . . "build it and they will come!" The place was so crowded patrons waited hours for their Bloody Marys! No one complained and once they received their Bloodys, they carefully carried the masterpieces to their seats. It was a huge success and people just couldn't stop talking about them.

Sarah Jayne now creates spectacular fundraising events centered around her Bloody Mary creations. After years of practicing and perfecting, Sarah Jayne began making lists of garnishes to adorn her own original Bloody Mary mix on her ever-present legal pad. Sarah Jayne makes her own Bloody Mary mix using over 35 ingredients including a hot sauce from Puerto Rico, a spice rub for corned beef from Ireland, a chipotle mix, a BBQ sauce with beer, tomato juices and other herbs that will remain her secret! She mixes and mulls all the ingredients together 4-5 days before adding strained and blended spices for an additional 2-3 days. Her standard recipe averages seven gallons which usually makes 150 Bloodys! Then Sarah Jayne sets out to design and shop for all the ingredients for the garnishes. She buys as much fresh and local as possible. This entire process takes about 1-2 weeks before she even starts prepping the mix and the garnishes. Her legal pad is full by this time with drawings, ideas, and ingredient lists. The major prepping is done the night before with an early morning set up at the event. Needless to say, Sarah Jayne does not sleep much during this process and usually needs

3-4 days to recuperate afterwards. But, it is her passion and those of us that are lucky enough to taste one of her creations are always delightfully thrilled! Sarah Jayne aspires to own her own bar and continue to amaze patrons with her culinary, artistic Bloody Mary creations and specialty cocktails.

You can still get a great Bloody Mary with 13+ garnishes at O'davey's in Fond du Lac. Hopefully you will be lucky enough to witness Sarah Jayne's magic if she's behind the bar serving up cocktails. But if you want a 'Sarah Jayne Bloody Mary Masterpiece' made with her own homemade mix, you will have to wait for her next fundraiser event!

Cheers to Sarah! Long may she reign as the Bloody Mary Queen!

scan me

Check out her Facebook page for Sarah Jayne sightings and events!

www.facebook.com/wildandcrazygourmetbloodymarys

MILLER PARK MAKES GREAT BLOODY MARYS

Miller Park is the home of the Milwaukee Brewers and THE place to get a really great Bloody Mary while watching the game from your seat in the stands! Delaware North/Sportservice Division operates Bloody Mary carts on the Field and Loge levels of the stadium. They create their Bloodys using Skyy Vodka and Ocean Spray Bloody Mary Mix (includes cranberry and tomato juice). It's served in a 20 oz. Brewers/Miller Park souvenir cup. But that's not all! With expert service provided by Dana Janik-Lemke and, up until this year, Julie Starks, your Bloody will be made to order, adding just the right amount of Tabasco®, Worcestershire sauce and celery salt to your liking. The cart service is all about 'the guest experience' and you will be treated like royalty when you step up to order your Bloody Mary. Without a doubt, the servers work diligently to "Make It Memorable" each time you visit their cart. That's what Brewers Baseball and Miller Park is all about . . . making memories!

You won't be disappointed with the garnishes on the Bloody Mary, either! Sure, they don't serve a burger or pizza slice on it, but you can get THAT and much more at the other vendors throughout the stadium. The Miller Park Bloody Mary comes with two olives, a pickle and a Usingers sausage stick! Perfect for at the ballpark. If you need a chaser, check out the many beer stands throughout the stadium. There are the usual Milwaukee beer standards, but Leinenkugels has multiple carts with many of their seasonal brews available for purchase.

There's no lack of food to go along with your Bloody Mary at Miller Park, where great food is served throughout the stadium! There's the usual hot dogs, brats, hamburgers and pretzels; but how about a huge loaded baked potato, beef brisket sandwich or a baseball helmet filled with deluxe nachos!!! New this year is the ever-delicious Smoke Shack with their pulled-pork sandwiches and AJ Bombers with their fully-loaded burgers. Check out the list at http://milwaukee.brewers.mlb.com/ballparks/stadium_maps.jsp?c_id=mil

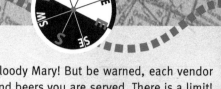

Why not try it all and have another Bloody Mary! But be warned, each vendor is very aware of how many Bloodys and beers you are served. There is a limit! They're only looking out for your best interest. They want you to enjoy the game and have a wonderful ballpark experience.

Now, you must know that my love for the Bloody Mary and Brewers baseball is big! But not as much as the newly-retired Bloody Mary server, Julie Starks! She has had a love affair with baseball all of her life and now that she has more time on her hands, she is planning to visit all of the ballparks in the U.S., including the minor league parks! Now that's dedication to the sport!

Julie started her career at Miller Park in 2010 working a variety of jobs, including wrapping hot dogs. She eventually found her home behind the Bloody Mary cart where she enjoyed talking with people and listening to the game. Not being able to see the game while she worked the cart never bothered her. She just enjoyed the atmosphere and being around baseball-loving people. Her technique for pleasing her customers was to make sure she got their names in the first minute guests approached her cart! Trust me, that is a plus when it comes to hospitality and Miller Park is BIG on guest services. As a Physical Education teacher in Milwaukee, Julie has the energy and the passion to work long hours at the ballpark after a day in the gym. That is true Brewers dedication.

Cheers to Julie and to all the servers at the Skyy Vodka Bloody Mary carts throughout Miller Park.

It's Bloodys, beer and baseball at its finest. With a high-scoring Bloody Mary, Miller Park really hit this one out of the park! Cheers Brewers Fans!

LISA LOVES BLOODY MARYS

I first met Lisa Collins at a book signing at the Kroghville Oasis in Waterloo, WI (one of the Top 10 Best Wisconsin Bloody Marys listed in my first book, *The Bloody Trail*). Lisa drove all the way from Oshkosh during a wicked Wisconsin snow storm just to meet me and buy an autographed book! Now that's dedication to the drink we both love.

Lisa is a Registered Nurse, but not a nurse in a uniform taking care of patients at a local hospital, which was something she loved doing for 25 years. Lisa is that calm, helpful voice on the other end of the phone when you make that frantic call for medical assistance or need advice on how to treat an illness. She has worked as a phone triage nurse for the last two years and she LOVES it. Every call is different which makes her job exciting and very satisfying as she helps many people every day with health issues or concerns.

Her love for her job is equal to her love for the Bloody Mary! Lisa started her Bloody Mary adventure while she was a nursing student at the University of Wisconsin-Oshkosh. Of course, it was THE hangover cure during her college years . . . isn't that true for most of us!? It wasn't until 2004 that Lisa started writing her own Bloody Mary notebooks. During her free time she traveled Wisconsin scoring Bloody Marys using her own rating system from 1 to 10. She took copious notes about each drink and why she did or did not enjoy them. Her travels have produced three thick pocket notebooks so far. Lisa has always been "in search of the perfect score" and enjoys the journey just as much as she enjoys Bloody Marys. And just like the calls Lisa receives at her phone triage job, she loves the search because "you never know what you're going to get!"

Her husband, two daughters, and her TWIN sister Kathy support her endeavor and enjoy the search right along with her. Her sister actually carries a celery stick in her purse in case the barkeep forgets to add one to her own Bloody! Lisa is known for carrying a bottle of Bloody Mary spices to use if the drink she's served doesn't have enough punch! When she orders her Bloody, she asks for two limes and tells the bartender to skip the Tabasco®. Lisa is definitely persnickety about her Bloodys, but I wouldn't want it any other way. She is unique and charming and I, for one, am happy she made that journey two years ago in the blizzard to meet me.

Here is Lisa Collins' best advice when it comes to scoring a Bloody Mary, "Judge a Bloody by how quickly you want to order another one!"

Cheers to you, Lisa Collins!
I am sure we will meet on
The Bloody Trail again!

THE BEN HIRKO STORY

And so it begins, a tale of one man's journey from dishwasher at a local restaurant to entrepreneur extraordinaire! This is the Ben Hirko Story. No, it's not a made-for-TV drama, this is a true story and I am pleased to tell you all about this man.

When Ben Hirko was 14 years old, he was hired at Nello's in Tempe, AZ as a dishwasher and busboy. He worked there for 4 years quickly moving up the ranks. At 18 years old, he felt qualified for the job, not only because he put in his time behind the scenes, but Ben was also the equipment manager at AZ State for 2 seasons and knew the importance of good management and teamwork.

When Ben was 20, he became the line cook at the Sports Column in Iowa City. His heavy schedule, 4pm to 2am/6 days a week, taught him that running a bar/restaurant business was hard work. But that didn't dissuade him from opening his own restaurant 7 years later. P'Sketti's Italian Restaurant in Liberty, IA, served spaghetti dishes 'fast-order style' something on the order of Qdoba. He provided customers with 4 types of noodles and 23 sauces to choose from! Ben found out the hard way that this was too much work for too little reward and closed shop after 2 years. Just another learning experience towards greatness!

Ben's struggles didn't end there. At 30 he quit a job as general manager at a fast-food restaurant in WI. He packed everything he owned into his mini-van with his dog riding shotgun. He was homeless with $900 to his name. He felt a failure. He moved back to IA and as if deja vu set in, was hired to cook and wash dishes at the Sports Column. During this time, Ben took "a 2-year vacation from life" to go back to school and to "reset his batteries". This plan served him well.

While at the Sports Column, Ben met the district manager at Sysco, who convinced him that he would make a great sales rep for their marketing division. So in February 2005, Ben started his new job. He was GREAT! He was named Rookie of the Year with phenomenal sales; however due to poor customer loyalty from some of his clients, Ben became frustrated. While at a hospital, awaiting the arrival of his first child, he found himself taking orders and dealing with customers during one of the most important days of his life. Ben decided at that moment that he was done! He left the food service industry completely and in February 2009 he started a lawn care business. As his own boss, Ben loved this business and he was very successful. During the winter months he would tend bar to keep himself occupied.

It was during one of his shifts, that a 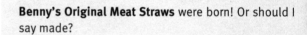 lit up! Two patrons of the bar, regulars on Wednesday nights from 6pm to 2am, would bring their own beef snack sticks with them to munch on while having their beers. Ben would serve them Bloody Marys and chat with them about this and that. They offered Ben a snack stick and Ben would stir his Bloody and take a bite. It was delicious! A perfect combination. Ben thought it would be even better if each bite would taste as good as the first one. So he took a plastic straw and began digging out the center of the snack stick to create a straw-like snack! It was AMAZING! He took his idea home and began working on a machine that would take the centers out of beef sticks to create beef 'straws'. After many failures and with the assistance of a mechanical engineer, the machine was made and patented!

Ben approached manufacturers in IA with his machine and product, but no one was interested. So he contacted a processing plant in another state and asked if he could present his idea to the owner. He drove 5 1/2 hours to the plant office to meet with him. The owner thought his idea was 'weird' but told Ben he would talk with the managers and get back to him in 3 days. Ben drove as far as Des Moines when he received a call that would change his and his family's life forever. The owner said that after seeing Ben's invention, everyone agreed, "Why not give this a try?!"

Benny's Original Meat Straws were born! Or should I say made?

For the first 6 to 8 months of production, Ben would drive his Nissan Pathfinder back and forth from IA to his processor to pick up 120-130 cases of packaged meat straws to fill the orders that were flying in once advertising went 'live' on his website in July 2011. Ben and his wife, Megan would fill all the orders out of their basement by hand.

What a great story, right? But wait! It's not over. In May of 2014, after many weeks of negotiation, Ben sold his patent and his business to DAS Foods, Inc., out of Palmyra, PA. The best part of the deal came when DAS Foods asked Ben to join their company as the sales rep for his own product! Ben was overwhelmed. He would still be a part of his 'baby' and enjoy seeing his idea become a big success. He sells his products throughout the country with the title, "National Account Manager for Benny's Bloody Mary Meat Straws". What could be better than that?!

This is truly AN AMERICAN DREAM story. Yes, their life did change in a huge way. But Ben, Megan, and now 2 children, Luke & Claire are ordinary people who have an extraordinary life due to hard work, perseverance, and a great imagination.

scan me

Now just how good are **Benny's Original Meat Straws?** They are fantastic, but "you don't have to take my word for it!" Visit **http://www.bennysoriginalmeatstraws.com/** and order your very own. You will not be disappointed. If you are, let me know and I'll buy you a Bloody! I am that sure!

Cheers to Ben Hirko!

FOREST FLOOR FOODS

A long time ago, a young man served our country as a Peace Corps volunteer in Thailand. Greg Floyd taught electrical/welding classes for 2 1/2 years to the local residents of Lampang. Fluent in the language, Greg often enjoyed visiting the volunteers from Germany who spoke English. He missed his native language and it was a treat to talk with them during his breaks. These fellows were teaching the local farmers how to grow mushrooms. Greg not only watched, he became totally enthralled with the idea. When he finished his tour in Thailand and came back home to Eden, Wisconsin, he told his parents that he wanted to start a mushroom farm. They supported his dream and Greg immediately went to Iowa to learn the trade. After five months, he returned to Wisconsin and rented space beneath the abandoned Ziegler Brewing Co., building in Beaver Dam. There were tunnels underneath the buildings which provided the perfect temperature for growing mushrooms. Greg leased the building from 1978 until 1980 when the building was scheduled to be demolished. He then built a state of the art facility in the township of Forest on part of his parent's farm near Eden. By 1981 he was growing a number of different varieties as the demand for fresh mushrooms increased. In 1990 his business, **GOURMET'S DELIGHT** became one of the 1st organic mushroom farms in the United States!

It was while Greg was being recognized for his mushroom farm that Peggy came into his life. She met Greg at a party and when he told her he was a 'mushroom farmer' she was smitten! It didn't take any convincing for Greg to fall for Peggy. His love of mushrooms and her love for the mushroom farmer would be the beginning of their love story and what would become their success story as well.

Forest Floor Foods
Pickled Products
EXPERIENCE THE FLAVOR

By 1995, Greg, Peggy and his brothers John and Rich, were knee-deep in mushrooms! Greg and Peggy sold their interest in the farm and began what is now FOREST FLOOR FOODS. Greg became a certified processor through a course in Madison. Peggy and Greg never took a pickling class, but developed their own recipes and their own 'art of pickling.' Pickling became their passion and mushrooms were their first experiment. They began with three flavors of mushrooms; Sour Cocktail made with vinegar, Dark Bergamo which are savory with oregano and pepper, and Classic Sweet almost like bread & butter; still the biggest seller in Wisconsin. In 1996 they debuted their products at the Midwest Specialty Food Show in Milwaukee and they won **BEST OF SHOW** and **BEST PACKAGING**. The Floyds had found their niche. Their new venture was thriving, but they quickly learned that finding distributors was the key to success when it came to getting the word out about their products. As their fantastic mushrooms and their pickling facility grew, their distributors and customers requested different veggies. By 2000, the pickled mushroom business was in full swing and Greg and Peggy were able to experiment with new products. Each new product can take up to 3-4 years to become popular. The Floyds understand the patience needed for this to work and their patience has paid off. Peggy has the final say in taste-testing and everything must meet her criteria. (I do love that word!) But, overall Greg and Peggy Floyd insist that all their products are FLAVORFUL, FRESH, AND CRUNCHY. All the pickling is done by Federal and State Standards right there in their pickling plant in Eden.

Okay, let's get to the really important pickled products that make Wisconsin Bloody Marys the best! Because the Floyds were aware of the increasing Bloody Mary market they began producing pickled veggies to garnish the cocktail. They also developed a Bloody Mary Rimmer Salt, Bloody Mary Seasoning Mix, and Bloody Mary Spicy Swizzle Stix. FOREST FLOOR FOODS also makes two varieties of Bloody Mary mixes, Original-mild, and Hot & Spicy! Both are made with 80% tomato juice and can sit on the grocery shelf or in your home bar for one year without separating! It's that good!

You can add all of their 26 pickled veggies to garnish your Bloody Mary including 12 varieties of Specialty Stuffed Olives! And don't forget those Bloody Mary Swizzle Sticks that Peggy designed herself . . . not too fat, not greasy, and just enough spice to tickle your tongue!

If you aren't thirsty yet, you must have a Bloody already in your hand! Greg and Peggy Floyd started FOREST FLOOR FOODS from the ground up . . . pun intended! Their love story is inspiring and I hope you remember it the next time you load your grocery cart full of their pickled products. Sample all of them and you will agree that the Floyds know what they're doing and appreciate your support.

Cheers to Greg and Peggy!

contact

➤ www.forestfloorfoods.com

☎ (920) 477-6009

FUN FACT N⁰ 1

If you look closely you will find FOREST FLOOR FOODS products in the Brad Pitt and Angelina Jolie movie, *Mr. & Mrs. Smith*. Approached by Hollywood, Greg and Peggy provided products for the movie set. In fact, Brad Pitt loved the olives so much they had to send more jars during the filming!

FUN FACT N⁰ 2

For a California celebration for a James Bond movie, FOREST FLOOR FOODS provided 198 jars of (martini) olives for the invitations. In order to enter the party, guests had to bring in their jar of olives as proof that they were on the guest list! Cheers to that!

HERE ARE SOME GREAT "MUST-SEE" RESTAURANTS ALONG THE BLOODY TRAIL THAT YOU JUST CAN'T PASS UP!

Let's face it, the Bloody Mary at Franks Diner in Kenosha doesn't score high, but it's only because there isn't a chaser! The taste is fantastic; it's served in a pilsner glass, has a nice ridge of celery salt on the rim, and it's stirred to mix their 'not so secret' ingredients—pickle brines in red pepper flakes, which give it some heat! You don't often see that in some finer restaurants.

But what Franks' Bloody lacks in veggies (just a pickle sitting gently across the glass) and a beer, it provides in the best atmosphere around, with a staff of wonderfully mischievous cooks and servers! They don't put up with pushy, crabby customers and they will tell you to leave if you get nasty! The total experience at Franks Diner will knock your socks off! There's nothing else like it, but let's start at the beginning of time.

In 1926, downtown Kenosha residents witnessed something very unusual . . . six horses pulling a diner down the street! Anthony Franks, founder of Franks Diner, paid $7,500 plus $325 shipping for the building, brought all the way from New Jersey on a railroad flat car. The structure was built by the Jerry O'Mahoney Company and Anthony had to have it once he read about it in a magazine. He added a dining room in 1935 and a larger kitchen in 1945. The Frank family hosted many celebrities throughout the years; The Three Stooges, Lawrence Welk, Bela Lugosi, and Liberace to drop a few names! The new owners, Kevin Ervin and Julie Rittmiller, have served up their famous garbage plate breakfasts to Guy Fieri (they were featured on Diners, Drive-ins and Dives), Mark Ruffalo, Badfinger band members and various Green Bay Packers.

What's truly unique about Franks Diner is the patience of their patrons. There are specific Rules to Follow (see their website for these instructions) for all customers standing in line to get a seat at the counter or at a much-sought-after booth. And when I say 'stand in line,' that is exactly what you have to do—rain, snow, sleet, whatever the weather—because there is often a line all the way down the street from the front entrance! It is a Franks Diner legacy to stand in line for a seat while inhaling the aroma of delicious food. This iconic restaurant has been featured in the *New York Times* and the *Wall Street Journal*. Franks Diner

is proud to have been voted Best Breakfast and Best Diner in Kenosha County 2011, 2012 and 2013!

Not only is the food fantastic and the crew entertaining, the atmosphere inside is always a hoot!

You never know what someone will do to get a seat or what one of the cooks or servers will do to lighten up the atmosphere . . . as if it needs it! There's a lot of sarcasm and good humor being thrown around all morning long. Don't be surprised if someone brings out a tray of tequila shots and begins with the cooks before serving them to anyone in line that wants one!

Oh . . . and about that Bloody? Well, while you wait in line (and you must be patient), you can order a Bloody. Best to stay hydrated while you drool at the great plates of food being served right in front of you. Trust me, veggies are not needed in this Bloody. You will get all the veggies you want from their famous GARBAGE PLATE breakfast! Each meal is made to order and once you decide what it is you want in your eggs, it will take a while

contact:

📍 508 58th Street Kenosha, WI 53140

🏹 www.franksdinerkenosha.com

📞 (262) 657-1017

to make it to perfection. Thus the Bloodys and the shots! They use three or five eggs (your choice) and mix hash browns, green peppers, onions, and as many meats as you desire or perhaps corned beef hash works best for you. Then they add five different cheeses, jalapeños, mushrooms and tomatoes. Yep! Go for it all and you will not be disappointed!

A visit to Franks Diner has to be on your Bloody Mary Bucket List! You will want to go back again and again just for the experience of it all. Cheers! Oh, and no whining!

What first catches your eye as you enter Stevens Point from the south is the beautiful wood building that looks like a train car. Well, that's because that is exactly what the Silver Coach is!

A beautifully crafted 1903 Smith & Barney railroad sleeper car that was purchased in the 1930s after the end of prohibition by John and Fred Bablitch. It was moved to its present location in the 1940s and was converted into a distinctive bar featuring its original stained glass and curved wood panelling with inlaid designs. Silver Coach has a rich history and is known as a 'hangout' for mobsters that were traveling through town. It was a small intimate bar with a piano for entertaining. One can just imagine what the subject of conversation was when the place was crowded with notorious patrons!

In 1955, owner Charles "Pete" Redfield added a dining room and began serving Cantonese food. Jim Gitter purchased the Silver Coach in 1987 and through the years restored the interior to its current beauty. The lower basement level still looks like it did in the 40s with remnants of a shuffleboard still on the basement floor! It is a magnificent piece of history.

In 2001, Chef Rob Tuszka and his wife Brenda purchased the restaurant and continued the tradition of unique, made-from-scratch flavors that the Silver Coach is known for. Chef Rob had always dreamt of owning his own restaurant after working as a chef for many years. He uses only the finest ingredients in all of his dishes. Chef Rob encourages customers to visit and experience their unique and tasty cuisine.The restaurant seats 70 and there are two private dining rooms just for two for those special occasions.

Oh, by the way, their Bloody Mary isn't bad either! They make their own mix and it has a unique flavor that can only be described as 'delicious'! The ingredients are a mystery but one can certainly see the horseradish! Add a $2 10 oz Spotted Cow (the only tap beer they have) and you have a great experience in front of you . . . just like their food . . . tasty and nutritious.

If you close your eyes you can imagine what it might have been like to travel along the rails across this great country. Of course it helps if you have a Bloody in your hand!

Cheers to Chef Rob and Brenda!

SILVER COACH
FRESH FOOD · FINE SPIRITS

contact

📍 38 Park Ridge Drive, Stevens Point

➤ www.silvercoachrestaurant.com

📞 (715) 341-6588

Referred by: Jason from the Joy Cardin radio program in December of 2013

When Owner/Chef Shane Valenti was just four years old and growing up Italian in a single parent household, he learned to cook soup and spaghetti to help his Mom. While she worked, Shane took care of his Uncle who was in a wheelchair. He remembers a childhood filled with cooking, large Sunday family dinners and watching Julia Child on TV while his friends played outside. He was passionate about food then and he never stopped learning. As an adult, Shane worked in the restaurant business for 16 years for Johnny V/RC Schmidt. This experience in the restaurant realm only strengthened his desire to own his own place.

Situated on the shores of Silver Lake, The Lakeside Supper Club has had a long history. For 60 years it was called Chuck's Supper Club and it was very successful. Unfortunately, the place burned down twice before the current building was constructed. The original concrete forms shipped from Germany are still visible in the basement. When The Lakeside went up for sale in 2010, Sean Burke bought it and Shane became the chef and partner in the business. In the next few years, Shane oversaw the renovation and updating of the kitchen and dining areas and he created his own menu. He used many recipes handed down from the previous owners, but while Shane wanted to maintain that classic 'supper club' feel, he wanted to give it a modern twist. Finally, in April of 2015, when everything was ready, Shane opened HIS restaurant, The Lakeside Supper Club and Lounge. The restaurant has a large dining room and outdoor patio, a U-shaped bar, and a dance floor and stage for live bands. Access to boaters and travelers alike, The Lakeside offers a great view and delicious food to weary travelers or boat enthusiasts. Shane has definitely found the right recipe for success as his patrons are the young and the young-at-heart.

Of course, The Lakeside Supper Club would not be in this book if it didn't have a tasty Bloody Mary! On weekdays and Saturdays, The Lakeside offers a pint glass of their delicious house-made Bloody Mary mix. The ingredients are kept a secret but this one definitely has a great taste. Shane also creates a "Bloody Mary of the Month" like his Green Bloody made with green tomatoes and various green veggies topped with a rosemary demi-glaze. All Bloodys are served with a 6 oz. beer chaser of your choice, and garnished with a summer sausage slice, three cheese curds, two olives, two mushrooms, a pepper and a pickle.

BUT WAIT! Come on a Sunday and you will be blown away! The Lakeside is known for its Bloody Mary Lazy Susan. This same delicious Bloody is transformed into a modern version of a supper club classic, "the deli tray." It is placed on a custom-made Lazy Susan board surrounded by whatever veggie was pickled that week, a cheese and sausage plate, pickled herring, or cheese-stuffed cherry tomatoes, or soft pretzels. You will get the same garnishes on the Bloody as usual and a 6 oz. beer; but to top it all off, a shot of whisky awaits each thirsty patron as well!

Now, that's what I call a blast from the past . . . beer, Bloody and whisky with snacks to match. Classic.

Keep up the good work! Cheers to Shane!

contact

📍 37238 Valley Road, Summit

➤ http://www.thelakesidesupperclub.com

📞 (262) 567-5242

In beautiful Superior, Wisconsin sits an unobtrusive building with bright blue awnings that match the waters of Lake Superior on a sunny day. Once you enter Anchor Bar you will be transported into the belly of a collector's dream. The bar is filled, and I mean FILLED, with nautical memorabilia that is outstanding, peculiar, and intriguing. You will not be bored waiting for your food which, by the way, is also outstanding! Anchor Bar only serves burgers and fries!

These are not just ordinary burgers though. They use one deep fryer and a small grill to prepare the most delicious burgers I have ever tasted! My personal favorite is the cashew burger with sautéed onions and yes, cashews!!!! C'mon! You have many burgers to choose from and each one is carefully cooked to perfection. With this small kitchen, you do have to be patient . . . but it is well worth the wait! This place is packed every day of the week with all sorts of characters from doctors, sailors, politicians, and truckers to families and college students.

Diners, Drive-ins and Dives from the Food Network did a piece on Anchor Bar in January of 2011, but they didn't need the publicity. Owners Adam and Aaron Anderson run the bar along with their manager, "Bean." They run it very smoothly and efficiently in order to keep their prices low—so eating here more than once a week won't hurt your wallet, and your stomach will be happy too! The Anderson brothers worked alongside their Dad, Tom, for many years until his sudden passing from cancer in 2008. They are keeping his memory alive by running the business in the same way "Tommy Boy" did. He is greatly missed by family, friends and the many patrons whose lives he touched every day.

contact

📍 413 Tower Avenue, Superior

↖ anchorbarandgrill.com

📞 (715) 394-9747

Here's a sampling of some of their burgers offered on a daily basis:

HAMBURGER
Plain but pleasant

CHEESEBURGER
You are in Wisconsin

SWISS BURGER
Lots of cheese but no mountains

BACON BURGER
Bacon, cheese, tomato

MUSHROOM AND SWISS
Self-explanatory

REUBEN BURGER
Sauerkraut and swiss

ANCHOR SUPREME
Slice of ham and cheese

CASHEW BURGER
Cashews and swiss

OLIVE BURGER
Green olives and cream cheese

BLUE CHEESE BURGER
Burger not really blue

JALAPEÑO CREAM CHEESE BURGER
Jalapeños with cream cheese

They're all under $7, and most under $5! Wow! Like I said, this place is worth the drive and well worth the wait.

Their cashew burger was named one of 101 Best Burgers in America by MSN in 2014 and Anchor Bar was featured in the book Hamburger America as one of 150 great burger joints in the U.S.A.

They do serve a tasty Bloody Mary with a chaser, but it just didn't meet my criteria. Go ahead and order one along with your burger . . . you won't be disappointed.

Cheers to Adam, Aaron and "Bean!"

Although I was there to have dinner, I did find a tasty treat that I had never heard of before. This fine dining restaurant located in the Chula Vista Resort in Wisconsin Dells served me a (are you ready for this?!) Bloody Mary Martini! I totally fell in love! It was delicious and looked so elegant served up in a martini glass with a pickle and two cheese-stuffed olives clinging to the rim! This Bloody Martini is composed of freshly squeezed lime juice, Tabasco®, Worcestershire sauce, and a "mysterious red ingredient!" Celery salt on the rim makes this the perfect sipping Bloody. Of course, if you so desire, they will serve a chaser with it, so it definitely qualifies as a Bloody Mary!!!

Kaminski's Chop House is known for their extraordinary steak dinners and HUGE portions of potatoes and vegetables brought to each table on a cart and graciously served by servers from all over the world. Chula Vista Resort hires young men and women from around the world who work various jobs at the resort including serving meals at Kaminski's Chop House. It is always a pleasure to speak to these young people and they are truly happy to be working in the United States. It shows on their faces and the way they treat their guests.

Kaminski's ad boasts, "In a state where meat eating is a religion, the devout have a new destination: Kaminski's Chophouse, a restaurant devoted to the sublime pleasures of hand-cut, dry-aged beef, well-chosen wines, and extraordinary service." And believe it, people; they do all that and more!

KAMINSKI'S
TRADEMARK
CHOP HOUSE

contact

📍 PO Box 30, 2501 River Road
Wisconsin Dells

➤ kaminskibros.com

📞 (608) 254-2001

THE BEST ON THE ROUTE

4TH BASE RESTAURANT
MILWAUKEE

There's a bar in West Allis, Wisconsin on National Avenue that is very unassuming, old-school style on the outside, but once you enter that front door you become the most important person on the planet! Or at least in the 4th Base Bar! Located just minutes from Miller Park, 4th Base hits a home run with every customer!

CJ Papara, the 2nd generation owner, assures me that "excellent personal service" is #1 at 4th Base. And I believe him! As you enter, you are greeted by the barkeep or CJ himself with a friendly welcome and "how are you?" The bar is decorated like a sports bar with baseball paraphernalia throughout, including helmets, bats, and photographs of sports stars past and present, but that's where it ends because 4th Base is much more than a place to hang out and watch Brewers baseball. It's your home away from home, a place to hang your hat, chill out and enjoy the friendly, warm atmosphere.

Before I get to their delicious Bloody Mary, here's some history of the place. 4th Base was opened in 1977 by CJ's Dad, Peter. Located in what was known as "Piggsville," the slaughterhouse district just south of the Wisconsin Avenue viaduct, the bar was a very popular place for great food and camaraderie. Unfortunately, too much rambunctious fun made the neighbors unhappy and Peter was forced to move 4th Base to it's present location on National Avenue. The building was already a bar, but the owner actually lived in the rest of the house.

What was once a living room has been turned into a cozy dining room for those patrons who prefer a fine dining atmosphere versus the bar scene. Same great food and same fantastic Bloodys are available no matter where you choose to sit!

Oh yeah, about their Bloody Marys! This 'always high-scoring' Bloody is

THE BLOODY SCORE

POINTS CATEGORY	SCORE
4 Glass	4
2 Celery salt	1
3 Shaken	3
10 Veggies	10
6 Presentation	6
15 Taste	13
10 BeerChaser	10
50 Total	47

A full 16 oz. beer!

over the top with flavor and garnishes. Each Bloody Mary is made ONE AT A TIME! Using Sacramento Tomato Juice as a base, each glass gets its very own concoction of horseradish, Tabasco®, Worcestershire sauce, celery salt and seven mystery spices. CJ prefers to use Gordon's Vodka because infused vodkas take away from the great taste of his Bloody mix and this patron strongly agrees. This is one tasty Bloody. Served in a pint glass, it is smothered with fresh (not pickled) yellow squash, green beans, snap peas, broccoli floret, asparagus, cauliflower, carrot and zucchini! Add two large olives and a pickle on a skewer made to look like a smile, and a pile of crispy onion rings and you have one heck of a great Bloody! But wait! It is served with a FULL-SIZE, 16 oz. BEER of your choice! No kidding!

And the food at 4th Base is amazing. They're all about fresh seafood, produce and meat purchased from local vendors. All of their entrees are made to order. When you are ready to order your meal, you visit their deli case at the back of the bar and choose what you want. Do you want a steak or chicken breast with a Portobello mushroom, or a shrimp or scallop or two or three . . . well, you get the picture! The 'cooks' (I prefer 'chefs' cuz they're that good) are experts at this technique. Antonio, "The Machine" has been doing this for over 10 years and you know he loves his job because each meal not only looks beautiful, it tastes amazing!

If you want it, you will get it! CJ's motto is "If it's good, they will wait for it!" That goes for the Bloody Mary and your great meal. Peter "Papa" Papara makes sure everything is good to go each morning. He arrives at 6 a.m. to set up the fresh, local produce and meats and gets the bar ready for that early morning arrival looking for a pick-me-up!

4th Base is the place to make yourself at home. It's all about the 'personal' experience and you will not be disappointed.

Cheers to CJ and "Papa" Papara!

RUSTY'S BACKWATER SALOON STEVENS POINT

The drive to Stevens Point, WI is a lovely one with many winding turns and beautiful scenery along the way. Once there, the city has some great stops— antique shops, art galleries, breweries and the UW campus. Just six miles southwest of the city, over more winding roads bordered by fir trees, is a quaint bar and grill settled along Mill Creek. Rusty's Backwater Saloon serves as a watering hole for those traveling by vehicle or boat. A dock set just yards from the front door of the saloon allows boaters to step off their crafts and into the bar. The owner of this hideaway is Rusty, who goes by one name only! He's had this nickname for 30 years and there's no changing it now!

The story of the saloon goes back to the 1940s when it was a small bar with eight stools called Kubishak's Resort. A gentleman named Leroy (Red) Phlugardt purchased the place in 1977 after the owners retired. Leroy renamed the bar, oddly enough, "The Red Snapper" (does everyone remember their history lesson?) Perhaps he named it for all the snapping turtles that lived in the creek nearby, or that may have been his nickname, but definitely not after Fernand Petiot's NYC cocktail! The bar mysteriously burned to the ground a month later, but Leroy built a new building and the place remained open until February 1985.

THE BLOODY SCORE		
POINTS	CATEGORY	SCORE
4	Glass	4
2	Celery salt	2
3	Shaken	0
10	Veggies	8
6	Presentation	6
15	Taste	13
10	BeerChaser	10
50	Total	43

On March 1, 1985, at the young age of 25, Rusty bought the property while he was working at a local paper mill. He had never tended bar but thought it might be an easy way to make money. He quickly learned that that was not the case, but he still enjoyed the idea of owning and running his own bar. He ran the bar for 10 years while still employed at the mill. He hired two bartenders the first year and added two more in the next couple of years as the popularity of the place grew. Using only a countertop fryer and a grill, Rusty served burgers for the first four years of operation. He did most of the cooking himself AND tended bar. Almost a 'one-man show!'

Of course all this talk about the saloon is great, but let's get to their high-scoring Bloody Marys! Rusty started experimenting making Bloody Marys just because he enjoyed drinking them. Once he bought the bar, it just seemed natural to serve his own creation to his patrons. He was surprised when everyone loved them as much as he did! According to Rusty, he and his staff have trained new bartenders for the last 14 years making sure they all make their Bloody Marys

RUSTYS
backwater saloon

the way RUSTY makes them! Served in a 20 oz. mug with a thick rim of celery salt, this Bloody is made in layers. First the ice, of course, then a squirt or two of mysterious hot sauce followed by vodka, Worcestershire sauce and more of that hot sauce. Topped off with V-8 juice, lots more celery salt and, if you have requested it, fresh crushed garlic right down the center for more spice! Then some pepperoncino peppers, banana peppers, a pickle and wait for it . . . a 12" sausage stick that is so big it leans over the rim of the mug! Add an 8 oz. chaser in either a jam jar or a tapper and you have yourself a mighty tasty Bloody Mary smack dab in the middle of nowhere!

Rusty wants to make sure his patrons are served great food, so when he started running the saloon he created his own menu items. Two of the most popular are the "Rusty Burger" with your choice of toppings, or the "Chicken What The Hell" sandwich that combines a juicy chicken breast with BBQ pork and lots of cheese melted on top! Rusty created this tasty sandwich one day after working at the bar. He couldn't decide if he wanted a chicken sandwich or a shredded pork sandwich so he said, "What the hell! I'm going to put them together!" Trust me, this one is delicious! Add deep-fried cheese curds or Rusty's fabulous french fries with your sandwich and you will be in love with this place. Rusty buys local as much as possible and insists that everything is fresh and made with the finest ingredients.

The road trip to Rusty's Backwater Saloon is well worth it but, of course, you MUST have a Rusty's Bloody Mary in front of you to enjoy the entire experience the proper way. Rusty is proud that his saloon has been open every day since March 1st, 1985 . . . that's approximately 11,000 days and still counting!

Here's to Rusty . . . Cheers my friend!

GOLDEN LAKE PUB

OCONOMOWOC   Referred by:
Wade and Jo Herman

Just on the border of Oconomowoc and Dousman, Wisconsin lies the beautiful, sandy Golden Lake. Golden Lake has a lot to offer. It is a great fishing lake with bass, perch, and bluegill, has great swimming with soft, sandy beaches and perfectly wonderful sunsets. Adding to this beauty is a sweet little pub located just yards from the shoreline, appropriately named Golden Lake Pub. The view from inside the pub allows patrons to watch boaters, kayakers, and nightly sunsets without leaving their seats! The pub owns 100' of frontage on the lake, 12 boat slips for rent on two piers, and a beach for patrons to enjoy their cocktails while taking in the scenery.

Taylor Shovick inherited Golden Lake Pub at the age of 19 when his father passed away. Taylor's Dad Rich had purchased the building from long-time owners Joy and Marty Liebling in 2005 as a real estate investment. After some renovating and updating, it was leased to a couple who had a bar business until 2010. In 2011, Rich passed from a heart condition at age 47 and his sister, Meribeth took over the books. As an accountant, Meribeth knew what would make this bar business successful and she tutored Taylor while the estate was settled. At that time, the township did not allow food to be served at the bar, but in

THE BLOODY SCORE

POINTS	CATEGORY	SCORE
4	Glass	4
2	Celery salt	1
3	Shaken	3
10	Veggies	10
6	Presentation	5
15	Taste	15
10	BeerChaser	5
50	Total	43

2014 that permit was provided and the Golden Lake Pub began their famous Sunday Brunch and Bloody Marys.

Taylor and Aunt Meribeth have created a welcoming oasis that brings in people from miles around for their Sunday Brunch menu which may include Pork Belly, Scotch Eggs, and Kitchen Sink Omelets! If you arrive after noon, you will be too late! Get there early and place your order and you will definitely enjoy the best brunch around along with their delicious Bloody Marys.

Served in a pint glass, their mix is quite unique. One of their sales reps introduced them to Big Kahuna Bloody Mary Mix made in Hawaii. As the bar's popularity grew and the demand for Bloodys increased, Meribeth and Taylor decided to use the Big Kahuna Bloody Mary Mix exclusively. Their rep could no longer provide them with the product, and it took Meribeth six months to find the company to order the mix directly. Now that's all they serve and everyone is happy! This mix is fantastic all on its own and I am surprised I haven't seen it served anywhere else! It comes in a carton and once their in-house pepper-infused vodka and celery salt have been added to the glass, the mix is poured right from the carton . . . unbelievably good!

This Bloody is treated with great garnishes: celery, asparagus, pepperoncini, pickle, olive, green bean, pepper, 2 mushrooms, 2 cheese cubes, 2 sausage cubes, tomato, a crispy onion ring and a cold shrimp. On Sundays they will throw on some bacon just for kicks! All this for $7.00. The Shovick's insist on consistency and they don't over fix or over pour. A perfect combination! The pub opens weekdays at 2 pm. Just the right time for that first Bloody Mary of the day! Open on Saturdays 11am and 9:30am on Sundays for brunch.

Cheers to Meribeth and Taylor Shovick!

CORNER POCKET
SPORTS BAR & GRILL   PORTAGE

Driving through Portage, Wisconsin is always a lovely experience. Of course, you are at the threshold of the Wisconsin Dells and the landscape is fantastic! Right smack in the middle of downtown Portage, at a busy intersection, is a resting spot you have to visit. It is the Corner Pocket Pub located in the Graham Building. Built in 1873, the Graham Building used to house a drugstore with a soda fountain (remember those?!). Upstairs were the offices of a doctor and a dentist. But before that, this location was notorious for where many criminals of high crimes and misdemeanors were hung from the telegraph wires along the dirt road going through town! Yikes! The tunnels between buildings are still in existence as well as a safe from the 1850s sitting in this building's basement. The stories it could tell!

THE BLOODY SCORE

POINTS CATEGORY		SCORE
4	Glass	4
2	Celery salt	0
3	Shaken	0
10	Veggies	10
6	Presentation	6
15	Taste	14
10	BeerChaser	10
50	Total	44

During the 1940-50s the building held a variety store and then a beverage store. It stood vacant for many years until the owners could no longer manage the mortgage. The bank repossessed it and that's when Mark Bellmore bought it and began to remodel the place.

It has great architecture and he wanted to highlight its beauty. It's been remodeled three times since that purchase until its' present design. The six huge pillars that stand throughout the main floor are made of cast iron and support the entire building. Mark had them painted to look like granite and no one knows the difference . . . I guess, until now! Mark rented out the newly renovated building up until 2006 to an insurance company, a title office, and a lawyer, until the recession hit. That's when the building became vacant once again.

Having no food experience Mark, his daughter Kelly and son Reid, decided that this building would be the perfect place to open a restaurant!

And why not?! They loved food, had some great ideas for their menu and Reid had a 'secret family recipe' for Bloody Marys. How could they lose? They originally started with six pool tables, but everyone was more interested in their great menu, so in the first week they removed four of them in order to put in more dining tables. Mark and his crew received a lot of assistance with their restaurant from mentors and suppliers. Their suppliers would critique their bar and food offerings and let them know what was popular at other venues. With Kelly working in the kitchen, Reid at the bar and Mark overseeing the entire operation, the Bellmore's have certainly created a great place for locals and tourists alike.

What makes Corner Pocket unique for this area is the large smoker located at its front entrance. The aroma coming from that smoker is so tempting, you just have to go in and get a taste of their fabulous smoked pulled pork! Definitely a winning combination, but let's get to why the Corner Pocket has one of the Top 10 Best Wisconsin Bloody Marys.

Their Bloody is not only made with Reid's 'secret family recipe' mix, and includes a 12 oz. beer of your choice, it also has delightful garnishes that make it one of the best. The mix has all the right seasonings with just the right amount of horseradish and Worcestershire sauce. Of course, who knows what else they

may have added! Garnished with a 10" sausage stick, asparagus, two olives, four mushrooms, and four pickle wedges, this Bloody is excellent! So get yourself to Portage and follow the aroma from their smoker as it carries you to their front door!

Cheers to Mark, Kelly and Reid!

THE HORSE & PLOW

KOHLER

There is a rich history to The Horse & Plow Bar and Restaurant. This historic tavern was constructed in 1924 as a recreation center and tap room for Kohler Co. workers who lived at The American Club. Dedicated on June 23, 1918, The American Club had a significant place in the development of Kohler Co. and Kohler Village. This example of a visionary concept of humanitarian interest in the worker can be contributed to Walter J. Kohler, Sr., during his tenure as president of Kohler Co. from 1905 to 1940. Kohler Co. is the worldwide leader in plumbing products and is still situated in the heart of the Kohler community.

THE BLOODY SCORE

POINTS CATEGORY		SCORE
4	Glass	4
2	Celery salt	0
3	Shaken	3
10	Veggies	10+2
6	Presentation	4
15	Taste	12
10	BeerChaser	5+2
50	Total	42

But, enough history. The real reason this establishment has been included in the Best Bloody list is due to their fantastic Bloody Mary. This Bloody is 16 ounces of made-to-order spicy goodness. One of their top bartenders will add horseradish on demand—or anything else for that matter! If it is not to your liking, she will start all over . . . but that won't happen, especially when you sample the mini salad bar expertly arranged on top! Named by Chef and Restaurant Manager Loren Rue, this "Mary of a Meal" includes a large celery stalk, lemon and lime slices, a skewer with a pickle, a pickled onion, two green olives, two

**44 HIGHLAND DRIVE
KOHLER, WI 53044**

920-457-8888

www.americanclub.com
www.facebook.com/TheHorseandPlow

mushrooms, an asparagus spear, a jalapeño pepper, and a brussels sprout! All of this for only $5.00 on Sundays!

Although the chaser is complimentary, it is only a 4-ounce beer. However you do have the astounding choice of 19 BEERS ON TAP, ranging from ales imported from Belhaven, Scotland, and Belgium and boasting 11 local brews from Wisconsin, including a root beer! To help you with this decision, any of their outrageous barkeeps will let you taste test those as well.

Enjoy your brew while lounging in the relaxing ambiance of nostalgic photographs from days gone by. Rest your elbows on tabletops that are made from the original American Club bowling lanes, which were located in the building where the bar now exists. Now that's a bit of bloody history! Cheers!

KITTY O'REILLYS IRISH PUB
STURGEON BAY

What would a Bloody Mary book be without including a true Irish pub? It would be blarney without one! Yes, there are many Irish pubs in Wisconsin; in fact, there are just about as many pubs as there are Irish people on St. Patrick's Day! Kitty O'Reillys Irish Pub in Sturgeon Bay has all the Irish spirits, including Guinness, Kilkenny, and Smithwicks, traditional Irish food, and live traditional Irish folk music/jam sessions (you can join in if you bring your instrument!) on the first and third Wednesday of each month, year round! Most importantly, my dear lass or lad, it has a good ol' Irish Bloody Mary that includes a chaser you can choose yourself from 12 different brews!

Yes, I can say it is an Irish Bloody Mary, because after the mix is poured into the 20-ounce goblet of ice, it is topped off with a bit o' Guinness! The pickled veggies are

THE BLOODY SCORE

POINTS	CATEGORY	SCORE
4	Glass	4+1
2	Celery salt	1
3	Shaken	2
10	Veggies	10+1
6	Presentation	6
15	Taste	13
10	BeerChaser	6
50	Total	44

great too and come with a Klement's Sausage and lots o' Renard's Mozzarella Whips layered on the top of the glass!

**59 E. OAK STREET
STURGEON BAY, WI 54235**

920-743-7441

www.kittyoreillys.com
kittyoreillys@gmail.com
@kittyoreillys

I must say that, even though we were enjoying our snacks in a glass, we just had to order some food from their great menu, which includes a Kilt Tilter Wrap, Irish Stew, Corned Beef and Hash, and Kitty's Cheeseburger topped with potato fries! O' yeah! All good!

Voted the "Best Happy Hour in Door County," Kitty O'Reillys offers drink specials every night along with 25-cent wings or $1 tacos or burgers, depending on the night. On Sundays, their Kitty's Loaded Bloody Mary is only $5.00! Of course, during Packer games, they provide free Jell-O shots every time the Packers score a touchdown! Go Green and Gold!

In true Irish tradition, Kitty O'Reillys website has a "Countdown to St. Patrick's Day" clock that counts down the seconds to next year's festivities. But with everything Irish they have to offer, every day at Kitty's is St. Patrick's Day. Their slogan is "Great Food, Great People, Great Spirits, Great Fun!" So go on in and join the fun! You don't have to be Irish to love this place!

BIG T'S SALOON

EAU CLAIRE
Referred by:
Randi and Rachel

Eau Claire, WI is a college town where bars are aplenty and Bloodys are found in almost every place. Yet, the Bloody Mary at Big T's Saloon on the corner of Vine and 3rd Street is the best!

It's a small bar that doesn't serve food, but they don't have to. The patrons come for the cozy atmosphere where the bartenders are friendly and well-trained at serving up cocktails and conversation. The building had a barbershop in the back room at one time, but its history as a bar dates back to the 1940's. It's a neat little building on a corner with an inviting front door and neon sign welcoming you inside.

In 2010, Terry "Big T" Luer purchased the Last Chance Bar and the building. He was very familiar with the place because he owned and had serviced all of the amusement devices in the bar for many years. He started his business, Video King in 1981 and basically took care of "anything that takes a quarter"! Born and raised in Eau Claire,

"Big T" grew up around the local neighborhood bars and as a kid aspired to eventually run his own buisness, which he did; and eventually own a bar, which he does! Two, in fact. His other bar, Big T's North Bar & Grill, is located in Cornell, WI at 116 Main Street. A modest man, "Big T" gives most of the credit to his bartenders, managers and customers, but the soul of his place definitely comes from "Big T" himself. This saloon is definitely a place to hang out and enjoy the company and of course, the Bloody Mary.

Big T's Saloon prides itself on consistency and that comes from "Big T's"own "goal in life" which was to create a great Bloody Mary the same way each and every time one is served. Each bartender is taught to make the Bloody precisely the same and patrons pay attention when theirs is being made. Not only is the mix homemade, each skewer of garnishes has to be built only one way so they will balance on top of the 16 oz. glass and placed facing the right direction! You will be amazed at how your Bloody looks when set in front of you.

When "Big T" decided Bloody Marys needed to be on the cocktail list he and several bartenders worked together to create a unique mix. Not only is the usual horseradish, Tabasco®, and Worcestershire sauce added to Clamato juice,

THE BLOODY SCORE

POINTS	CATEGORY	
4	Glass	4
2	Celery salt	0
3	Shaken	3
10	Veggies	10
6	Presentation	6
15	Taste	14
10	BeerChaser	8
50	Total	45

Big T's Saloon has its very own mix of spices that's sprinkled on the ice before anything else is added. Then they add pickle juice and their own recipe of asparagus and olive juice mixed with mushroom juice. It may sound crazy, but it tastes delicious! They keep the juices in separate squirt bottles and watching them mix it up in the pint glass is always a treat. Of course, they do a great job of shaking the drink before garnishing. That is a must to get a good score!

The garnish is amazing with just the right selection of goodies: a mozzarella cheese cube, colby jack cheese cube, a beefstick, Bergamo mushroom, sweet and sour pickle wedge, garlic olive, a pickle, orange pepper, 1/4" cucumber slice, radish, cherry tomato, scallion, celery stick, bacon strip, a shrimp, a ham flatbread sandwich slice topped with a tomato and olive, and this one had a Laffy Taffy candy for dessert! (Don't forget to read the joke!) On special occasions and holidays you may find a tasty muffin or cookie or some other baked treat on top of your garnish. A perfect ending to a great Bloody Mary. They added a ranch dressing cup on the side of their Bloody and have found that most everyone now eats the celery!

"Big T" buys most of his products from Sam's Club and Aldi's and the beef sticks come from Barney's Meat Market in Weyerhauser, WI. The skewers are put together with the garnishes in the same order, with over 100 made on any given Sunday!

Their Bloodys are served every day, but on Sundays those fully-loaded skewers are served from 6 am to 6 pm. So get there early before the skewers are gone! If you notice a guy behind the bar smiling at you as you devour your Bloody Mary, not to worry, it's just "Big T", Terry Luer, watching you enjoy his creation!

Cheers to "Big T" and his staff! **75**

SAYNER PUB
SAYNER

Traveling through Northern Wisconsin is always a beautiful ride, especially in fall when the colors are changing. It's even more special when you can find a spot to relax at with a great Bloody Mary! Sayner Pub is that spot. Set in the middle of Hemlock Forest State Natural Area and Bittersweet Lakes State Natural Area, Sayner Pub is a great place to take a break from driving all those winding, pine tree lined roads omnipresent in Northern WI. Located right on U.S. Hwy 155, you won't miss it on your way south.

The bar/restaurant is located in a building that has been the "Sayner Pub" since 1945. It was once owned by the Worthen family and then operated by Chris Hadrada. In 2004 the current owner, Eric "Liebo" Liebenstein, purchased the bar and created his own menu. The place was already locally famous for it's wings and pizza, and you can still get those items, but Eric added bar food, delicious entrees and a Friday Fish Fry. The menu also boasts about their 'Pub's Legendary Steak sandwich.' Patrons can eat at the bar, where you'll find a large, hand-painted map of the Sayner area and the many surrounding lakes of this region, or in their large dining room where you can enjoy your meal while watching the Packer game on strategically placed TVs. Of course, their high-scoring Bloody Mary is the highlight of your visit. After all, isn't that what you came for!!!

Eric "Liebo," worked at Sayner Pub for a year under the prior owner's management and, when the business was listed for sale, he jumped at the opportunity to run his own pub and create the atmosphere he knew would be successful. When Eric brought his palate to the menu, he also created something the bar didn't necessarily feature before; a fabulous Bloody Mary with a homemade mix. His recipe starts with Sacramento tomato juice but,

THE BLOODY SCORE

POINTS CATEGORY	SCORE
4 Glass	4+1
2 Celery salt	1
3 Shaken	3
10 Veggies	9
6 Presentation	5
15 Taste	14
10 BeerChaser	6
50 Total	43

(4 Times!)

as Jake, the General Manager explained, "we add a dash of this, a splash of that, and a squeeze of something else!" Well, whatever they are doing, it definitely works! To make sure this Bloody is over-the-top, Sayner Pub serves it in a 22 oz. mug with a 4 oz. chaser! With high-quality garnishes including a large, pickled mushroom, a sausage stick, and pepperjack cheese, this Bloody makes the perfect snack before your meal arrives.

Jake Long started working at Sayner Pub as a teenager. First, as a busboy, then a dishwasher, waiter, bouncer, and bartender. He even tried his hand as a cook, but he didn't care for that too much! As General Manager, you will find Jake behind the bar making sure your cocktails are served perfectly and promptly.

If you want to dine at the bar or in their large dining room, you are sure to get great service with a smile!

Cheers to Eric "Liebo" Liebenstein and Jake Long for making a great Bloody Mary deep in the Northwoods!

SIDE BAR

Jake's Grandpa Neal painted the two murals located on the walls above the bar. A long-time resident of Sayner, Grandpa Neal wanted to give travelers a birds-eye view of the many roads and lakes in the area. Even though it was painted in 1959, the mural provides an overview of the landscape of the area that still exists today. On the other side of the wall Grandpa Neal painted the "Mus-ski" Mountain. This was a ski hill active during the 50s, but it closed shortly after the painting was completed. At the base of the painting is an image of a couple with three small children; Jake's grandparents and their three sons. In another section of the painting there's an image of a tall man in a long jacket whom Grandpa Neal claims is Carl Eliason; the man who invented the snowmobile right here in Sayner, WI. Toast a salute to Grandpa Neal, Carl and the snowmobile! It's the right thing to do while sitting at the bar with your Bloody Mary.

MULLIGANS SPORTS BAR
& GRILL MOUNTAIN

Mulligans Sports Bar & Grill is located right off the ATV and snowmobile trails of Mountain, Wisconsin. The building was built in the 1930's as a train station for traveling loggers. Once called Joe's Place, it served as a boarding house where weary travelers could get a hot meal and a drink of Kentucky moonshine!

Purchased by Don and Pam Demmith in 1998 and officially renamed 'Mulligans Sports Bar & Grill' when they opened their doors in 2003, the place still serves hungry travelers and sportsmen all year round. The name 'Mulligans' comes from the saying, "do over without penalty" and that's how the Demmith's live. They enjoy serving their customers and it shows in the quality of their food and drinks, and the efficiency of their service.

THE BLOODY SCORE

POINTS CATEGORY		SCORE
4	Glass	4
2	Celery salt	1
3	Shaken	2
10	Veggies	10+1
6	Presentation	5
15	Taste	14
10	BeerChaser	6
50	Total	43

Pam knows the bar business well and has been a bartender since she was 16. She started her bartending career at Dobbert's Resort on the Wolf River. She brings her expertise to the bar each and every day. Her husband Don and three children all contribute to making sure every guest is served with a smile. Their menu has something for everyone from hot wings with 15 different levels of heat to salads, sandwiches, wraps, burgers, seafood, TexMex, and their very popular homemade pizzas! Bring the family! This place has a Friday Fish Fry you won't forget.

What makes this place tops is not only the friendly, fast service and the great food; it's their fantastic Bloody Mary! On any given day, Pam may serve up to 100 Bloody Marys, especially during the summer months. Her homemade mix with special, secret ingredients is made fresh every week; 10 gallons at a time

during the summer months and 15-20 gallons just in July alone! Now that's a lot of Bloodys! I know why . . . this Bloody is amazing and the garnishes are out of this world. But, remember, it doesn't matter what's on top as long as the cocktail has the right flavor. Pam serves her "sweet, tangy with just a little kick" Bloody Mary in a 24 oz. cup with 19-22 garnishes nestled on top. Served with a 5 oz. beer chaser of your choice from any of their 10 tap beers, this Bloody is just right after a long ride to the Northwoods in your car, motorcycle, snowmobile or ATV. Winter or summer, Mulligans never stops serving its' guest topnotch food and drink. After all, it's a tradition up here. Pam, Don and family would like to invite everyone to try their Bloody Marys anytime of the year either on their outdoor patio, at the bar, or by the fireplace in the dining room. There's plenty of room for everyone at Mulligans.

Cheers to Pam, Don and family!

WEST ALLIS CHEESE
AND SAUSAGE SHOPPE   WEST ALLIS

Referred by: Richard Van Egtern

You may think I've had one too many Bloodys, but YES, the West Allis Cheese & Sausage Shoppe is one of the Top 10 Best Bloody Marys in Wisconsin. But, let me explain myself first before I get to their Bloody Mary and why it's so darn good.

In 1968 when owner Mark Lutz was a kid living in West Allis, he remembers stopping in the Merkt's Cheese Store to buy candy and a beef stick on his way home from school. As the Merkt's company grew, the store became too small for manufacturing and distributing and they moved to a new location. The building became the West Allis Cheese & Sausage Shoppe and was owned by a local family for 18 years. Mark still visited the store often as an adult, but during the Christmas holidays in 2001, Mark found the doors closed. He was curious and called the owners. He found out the couple just could not run the place any more as health issues prevented them from managing the store. Mark asked about buying the business, but their first response was a loud "NO!" Mark was persistent and they finally agreed to sell him the place as long as he agreed to keep his engineering job just in case the business failed. They told him the location was not ideal and that it was a tough business to get into. Their honesty was appreciated, but Mark knew he could make this business a success. The first year they were opened, sales were low and Mark was concerned. He spoke with his contacts, distributors and customers to find out what was needed to keep the doors open. At this point in time, Mark still had his mechanical engineering job just as he had promised the former owners. His family ran the business while he was at work, making this family-owned-and-operated venture a success!

It wasn't until 2005, when Mark opened a branch of the West Allis Cheese & Sausage Shoppe in the Milwaukee Public Market on Water Street that things began to look up for the business. He was finally seeing success at both locations until an unfortunate accident occurred in 2007. The entire interior of the shop in West Allis burned down due to an electrical fire. Because the building was made of solid brick it was deemed safe, so Mark decided to rebuild bigger and better. The success of the 2nd location and it's restaurant/sandwich shop enabled Mark to rebuild and add new equipment to the original location. In 11 months time, the West Allis Cheese & Sausage Shoppe reopened. In 2013, with the success of the shop in downtown Milwaukee, Mark decided to add a cafe to the West Allis location with a sandwich menu and breakfast options as well. Mark knew this area of town needed a restaurant that would service the locals

THE BLOODY SCORE

		SCORE
4	Glass	3
2	Celery salt	1
3	Shaken	1
10	Veggies	9
6	Presentation	6
15	Taste	14
10	BeerChaser	10
50	Total	44

while providing the same cheese, sausage, wine, beer and bakery it was always famous for. The Cheese Shoppe gave a new perspective to this lovely West Allis area and brought pride to the community often overlooked by travelers and locals alike. Mark had 'made his mark' in the cheese & sausage business and I know first-hand why; he and his crew serve up fantastic sandwiches with a friendly 'hometown' atmosphere that is not often found in a big city.

So, back to the beginning . . . YES, they do serve a fabulous Bloody Mary with a homemade mix. Mark states that his mix does include Tabasco®, tomato juice, celery salt, and his favorite, a horseradish base. It's not too spicy, because as Mark states, "I like heat, but I don't like to be in pain!" His 'secret' ingredient is not so secret any more . . . he uses Colonel Pabst Worcestershire Sauce in his mix exclusively. (See Side Bar) It's a homemade sauce that makes the perfect match with his Bloody Mary mix and he wouldn't have it any other way! Not only is his Bloody tasty, the garnishes are just what you'd expect from a cheese and sausage shop. They include the usual olive, pickle and celery stalk, but then Mark adds a thick slice of Nueske's bacon, a 1/4 of a delicious grilled cheese sandwich, and a pile of mozzarella whips wrapped around all of it! Alongside this Bloody Mary served in a mason jar, is a Rhinelander Shorty! You can't complain about that. All in all, great service, great food, and a great Bloody on any day of the week is just what you can expect at the West Allis Cheese & Sausage Shoppe.

OnMilwaukee.com just named the West Allis Cheese & Sausage Shoppe a great alternative brunch spot, so I know what I'm talking about! It is a family owned and operated business with Mark, his wife Linda, daughter Hannah, and brother Howard ready and willing to serve their always happy customers.

Cheers to the Lutz family!

COLONEL PABST ALL-MALT AMBER LAGER WORCESTERSHIRE SAUCE

West Allis Cheese & Sausage Shoppe boasts its exclusive use of Colonel Pabst Worcestershire Sauce. Made from fresh Milwaukee all-malt lager and 21 all natural ingredients from around the world, including Indian tamarind, Grenadian ginger and Madras curry, this sauce brings a flavorful addition to your Bloody Mary or any other recipe you have in mind.

Colonel Pabst Worcestershire Sauce is small-batch brewed, bottled, and aged to perfection. The history behind the recipe goes back to Colonel Gustave Pabst, great-grandfather of Kate Quartaro, the owner of Colonel Pabst Worcestershire Sauce. Gustave was the eldest son of Captain Frederick Pabst, founder of the Pabst Brewery. Gustave was the first Pabst to be educated as a Master Brewer and the 2nd president of the Pabst Brewing Company when he took over the brewery in the late 1800s. His loyal friends included Adolphus Busch, Fred Miller, Val Blatz, Adolph Coors, Adam Gettleman and Johanna Heileman. Famous names I am sure many of you recognize! Gustave was chosen to represent the United States Brewers Association and became its' most outspoken voice in Washington D.C. in the fight against the 18th amendment . . . prohibition.

He was also an avid animal lover, donating to many zoos; a fan of children, donating to many orphanages, and a gentleman farmer and sportsman. He was praised by Aldo Leopold for importing upland game birds from around the world, some of which are still prevalent in the U.S. today.

The recipe for this Worcestershire sauce goes back a long way in the Pabst family's history. Kate Quartaro's mother, Elsa, was raised by her grandparents. She is now 80 years old and while cleaning out her cookbooks with Kate, she came across a recipe for Worcestershire sauce. Elsa's grandmother Hilda possibly created this recipe while visiting Gustave in Washington D.C. During this time of prohibition, many provisions were cut off from those living in the south. Southerners had to be creative when it came to making sauces and one of those sauces used beer! In fact, in the Pabst family, as well as many families during this time, using beer was pretty standard. Finding this recipe for Worcestershire sauce was not only a surprise, but an inspiration. Kate decided to 'whip up a batch' and give bottles of the homemade sauce to family and friends as gifts. It was so well-received that everyone insisted she should start bottling and selling it in retail stores. Kate began making small batches in her own home, but when sales exceeded her ability to keep up, she found a local facility with large brewing kettles and a bottling capability to craft-brew and bottle her sauce for her. It took over a year working with the company to duplicate the family recipe. It was a labor of love and the final product definitely proves that! Using ingredients from all over the world and a local brewery to provide the all-malt lager, Colonel Pabst Worcestershire Sauce is definitely unique and delicious. Its uses are endless, but we are talking about Bloody Marys here. This sauce makes for a rich, tasty Bloody; but don't take my word for it, go to West Allis Cheese & Sausage Shoppe and taste for yourself.

Cheers to Kate, Colonel Pabst, Hilda, and Elsa for carrying on a tradition we can now all enjoy!

THE BLOODY MAP

1. **4th BASE RESTAURANT**
   West Milwaukee

2. **RUSTY'S BACKWATER SALOON**
   Stevens Point

3. **GOLDEN LAKE PUB**
   Oconomowoc

4. **CORNER POCKET SPORTS BAR & GRILL**
   Portage

5. **THE HORSE & PLOW**
   Kohler

6. **KITTY O'REILLYS IRISH PUB**
   Sturgeon Bay

7. **BIG T'S SALOON**
   Eau Claire

8. **SAYNER PUB**
   Sayner

9. **MULLIGANS**
   Mountain

10. **WEST ALLIS CHEESE & SAUSAGE SHOPPE**
    West Allis

Superior

Hayward

8

9

Wausau

7

Eau Claire

2

Stevens Point

6

Green Bay

Appleton

La Crosse

Fond du Lac

5

4

3

10

1

Madison

Milwaukee

HONORABLE MENTION PAGE

Now just because your favorite bar or restaurant did not get chosen as one of the Top 10 Bloody Marys in Wisconsin for this book, don't be sad. There are plenty of great Bloodys to be found here, there and everywhere in this wonderful state of Wisconsin. Where better to find THE most delicious Bloody Marys with THE most outrageous garnishes than right here in good ole Wisconsin!

Here are some of those Bloody Mary establishments that, even though they were tasty, their Bloodys just didn't meet my criteria. You may not agree with me and I am OKAY with that! (Remember, this IS about enjoying Bloody Marys!)

DEL'S BAR IN LA CROSSE

SPRING BROOK SPORTS BAR IN WISCONSIN DELLS

MORTON'S IN CEDARBURG

THE LAKESIDE SUPPER CLUB IN SUMMIT

SILVER COACH IN STEVENS POINT

SHARKZ BREWZ & BITEZ IN GREEN LAKE

SAZZY B IN KENOSHA

THE SLINGERHOUSE IN SLINGER

THE WEARY TRAVELER FREEHOUSE IN MADISON

KROGHVILLE OASIS IN KROGHVILLE

THE WICKED HOP IN MILWAUKEE

SOBELMAN'S IN MILWAUKEE

OSCAR'S PUB AND GRILL IN MILWAUKEE

CUBANITAS IN MILWAUKEE

HOUDINI'S ESCAPE GASTROPUB IN APPLETON

TJ'S HARBOR RESTAURANT IN OSHKOSH

KAMINSKI'S CHOP HOUSE IN WISCONSIN DELLS-BLOODY MARY MARTINI

ANCHOR BAR AND GRILL IN SUPERIOR

LOADED SLATE IN MILWAUKEE

BIBLIOGRAPHY

Cole, Adam. "Cocktail Chemistry: Parsing the Bloody Mary." NPR. N.p., n.pag., n.d. Web.

Da Costa, Neil C. "Creating the Perfect Bloody Mary: Good Chemistry of Fresh Ingredients." American Chemical Society. N.p., Mar. 2011. Web.

Harrysbar. N.p., n.d. Web.

MacElhone, Harry. Harry's ABC of Mixing Cocktails. London: Souvenir Press, 1996. Print.

Nalley, Richard. "Legends of Old King Cole at the St. Regis." Forbes n.d.: n.pag. Web.

Roettger, Sarah. "The History of the Snit." Brunchkateers. N.p., 04 Feb. 2012. Web.

Smal, Alejandro. "How to Mix a Bloody Mary in 6 Steps."Facebook. N.p. May 2013. Web.

Thrillist. N.p., n.d. Web.

Tooke, Greg. "Bloody Mary Garnishes, Garnouflage?" Bestbloodmaryrecipe. N.p., n.d. Web.

Tooke, Greg. "7 Ways To Ruin a Bloody Mary." Bestbloodmaryrecipe. N.p., n.d. Web.

Wikipedia. Wikimedia Foundation, n.d. Web.

KEEP TRACK OF YOUR OWN BLOODYS HERE!

Score your finds and save 'em for future reference

BAR / RESTAURANT & LOCATION

COMMENTS

POINTS	CATEGORY	SCORE
4	Glass	
2	Celery salt	
3	Shaken	
10	Veggies	
6	Presentation	
15	Taste	
10	BeerChaser	
50	Total	

BAR / RESTAURANT & LOCATION

COMMENTS

POINTS	CATEGORY	SCORE
4	Glass	
2	Celery salt	
3	Shaken	
10	Veggies	
6	Presentation	
15	Taste	
10	BeerChaser	
50	Total	

BAR / RESTAURANT & LOCATION

_____

COMMENTS

_____

_____

_____

_____

_____

_____

_____

THE BLOODY SCORE

POINTS	CATEGORY	SCORE
4	Glass	
2	Celery salt	
3	Shaken	
10	Veggies	
6	Presentation	
15	Taste	
10	BeerChaser	
50	Total	

BAR / RESTAURANT & LOCATION

_____

COMMENTS

_____

_____

_____

_____

_____

_____

_____

POINTS	CATEGORY	SCORE
4	Glass	
2	Celery salt	
3	Shaken	
10	Veggies	
6	Presentation	
15	Taste	
10	BeerChaser	
50	Total	

KEEP TRACK OF YOUR OWN BLOODYS HERE!
Score your finds and save 'em for future reference

BAR / RESTAURANT & LOCATION

_____

COMMENTS

POINTS	CATEGORY	SCORE
4	Glass	
2	Celery salt	
3	Shaken	
10	Veggies	
6	Presentation	
15	Taste	
10	BeerChaser	
50	Total	

_____
_____
_____
_____
_____
_____
_____
_____

BAR / RESTAURANT & LOCATION

_____

COMMENTS

POINTS	CATEGORY	SCORE
4	Glass	
2	Celery salt	
3	Shaken	
10	Veggies	
6	Presentation	
15	Taste	
10	BeerChaser	
50	Total	

_____
_____
_____
_____
_____
_____
_____
_____

CPSIA information can be obtained
at www.ICGtesting.com
Printed in the USA
BVHW021033281021
619993BV00001B/27

* 9 7 8 1 9 4 3 3 3 1 1 2 3 *